Field Guide to Wild Mushrooms
of Pennsylvania and the Mid-Atlantic

Field Guide to Wild Mushrooms

of Pennsylvania

and the Mid-Atlantic

Bill Russell

A Keystone Book™

The Pennsylvania State University Press
University Park, Pennsylvania

A Keystone Book™ is so designated to distinguish it from the typical scholarly monograph that a university press publishes. It is a book intended to serve the citizens of Pennsylvania by educating them and others, in an entertaining way, about aspects of the history, culture, society, and environment of the state as part of the Middle Atlantic region.

Unless otherwise noted, all photographs are the author's own.

Library of Congress Cataloging-in-Publication Data

Russell, Bill, 1935–
    Field guide to wild mushrooms of Pennsylvania and
    the Mid-Atlantic / Bill Russell.
        p.   cm.
Includes bibliographical references and index.
ISBN 0-271-02891-2 (pbk. : alk. paper)
1.   Mushrooms—Pennsylvania—Identification.
2.   Mushrooms—Middle Atlantic States—Identification.
I.   Title.

QK605.5.P4R87 2006
579.609748—dc22
               2006006628

Designed by Regina Starace
Printed in China through C & C Offset
Published by The Pennsylvania State University Press,
University Park, PA 16802-1003

Fifth printing, 2016

The Pennsylvania State University Press is a member of the
Association of American University Presses.

WARNING

There are risks involved in consuming edible wild mushrooms. To minimize them, it is necessary to obtain positive identification of each mushroom, to collect the proper mushroom structure at the correct stage of development during the proper season, and to prepare it in a specific manner for consumption. Even though these steps may be followed exactly, the possibility exists that the consumer may be allergic to the mushroom or that the mushroom may in some way be anomalous. The author has been conscientious in his efforts to alert the reader to potential hazards of consuming edible wild mushrooms, but the reader must accept full responsibility for deciding whether to consume any particular edible wild mushroom.

The descriptions of medicinal uses of wild mushrooms given in this book are for educational purposes only. The author is not recommending the use of these mushrooms in self-medication. Always consult a physician about such use.

This book is not intended to be used as the sole source for mushroom identification.

Contents

Preface

How far back can your memory reach? If I really stretch, my earliest memory is of hunting mushrooms as a toddler with my parents, early on a misty summer morning, in an old graveyard near our home. Mushrooms grew everywhere. To me, they looked like big white buttons hiding in the grass. My parents carried tomato baskets and kitchen knives. Because I was so small—and thus close to the ground—I spotted a few tiny ones that my parents had overlooked. Afterward, I sat in my high chair near the kitchen table, impatiently waiting while my mother cooked the mushrooms we had brought home. She served me a little dish with three small sautéed button mushrooms—the mushrooms that I had found. To this day, I remember the earthy, sweet taste. From that moment I became hooked on mushroom hunting.

After I learned to read, my father bought me a wild mushroom identification book. Over the winter I memorized many of the mushroom descriptions. The following summer I studied the mushrooms that were growing in the woods, fields, and backyards around my home. My parents knew only one edible mushroom species (the one that grew in the graveyard), which they called a field mushroom. No one else in the area knew any others. I realized that if I wanted to discover other edible mushrooms, I would have to do it on my own.

Discover them I did. The first edible mushroom I identified by myself, with enough certainty to sample, was the glistening inky cap. Because it appeared in large crops in my backyard several times a season, I had plenty of opportunities to examine it closely and consider its edibility. The first time I ate it, I followed the advice in my book and sautéed a small sample. It was delicious, with a flavor very different from those of the supermarket white button mushrooms and the field mushrooms. I was eager to learn more about edible mushrooms, but I knew that it was important to move ahead slowly and carefully. Within a couple of years, I learned on my own to identify several edible species confidently.

My parents constantly felt torn between encouraging their budding mushroom hunter and saving their lives. Thanksgiving Day marked the beginning of velvet stem mushroom season where we lived. Lots of them grew on a log pile in the woods not far from the house, and every year I gathered a big basketful for the turkey stuffing. Every Thanksgiving morning, I would bring the basket into the bustling kitchen and proudly announce that I had the mushrooms for the turkey stuffing. Every year I would be greeted with silence. Yet every year I went ahead and stirred the velvet stems into the turkey stuffing mix. When dinner was served later in the day, a mountain of stuffing covered my plate. For days after, I had stuffing for breakfast, stuffing sandwiches for lunch, and warmed-over stuffing for dinner. Every year I had all the Thanksgiving turkey stuffing I could eat—because no one else would eat it.

By the time I graduated from high school, I had learned to pick about fifty edible mushrooms. Then, as an undergraduate physics student, I made a wonderful discovery: the University library had a huge collection of mushroom books. Over the next four years I learned about dozens of other edible mushrooms. A year after graduation, I began an extended period of postgraduate studies in the biological and botanical sciences that further expanded my knowledge and understanding of mushrooms.

There's no end to learning about mushrooms. You could study them over several lifetimes without knowing everything there is to know about them. My mushrooming friends and I get together several times a year to share each other's knowledge and experiences. You can do the same. Form a circle of friends who are interested in mushrooms, and you will all learn faster. To meet other mushroom enthusiasts, you may want to check out the North American Mycological Association. Find them on the Internet at www.namyco.org.

The difficulty of reading a mushroom guide often puts off a beginner. To make it easier, I have avoided using many technical terms in the mushroom descriptions. You don't have to be a botanist in order to use this book. You only need to have an interest in nature and the willingness to look closely at the mushrooms growing around you. You will discover that certain mushrooms are easy to identify, while others need your time and attention. With a bit of dedication, you should soon be able to name many of the wild mushrooms that you meet in your backyard, on your walks, and on your outings. You will also find directions for transplanting wild mushrooms into your backyard, suggestions for gathering and using certain species, and fun things to do with mushrooms. Even experienced mushroomers will benefit from the tips and personal observations I offer based on many years of mushrooming.

This book is not intended to be your only guide to identifying, gathering, and using mushrooms. To learn a new mushroom, you need to become a detective, gathering clue after clue from your observations and from mushroom books that will lead you to a positive identification of the species. It's well worth the effort to seek out a knowledgeable teacher. But when your teacher is not available, you will have to rely on as many mushroom guidebooks as you can get your hands on. Each author has his or her own photographs, illustrations, descriptive details, and comments that will help you, and experienced mushroomers know that all sources of clues are important. The more information you have, the better. Try my website www.brussellmushrooms.com

Happy mushrooming!
WILLIAM E. (BILL) RUSSELL

Acknowledgments

I wish to express my thanks to Anne Quinn Corr for getting the ball rolling; Ken Klein for his wise feedback; Karen Martin for her friendship and knowledgeable comments; Geraldine S. Russell for her encouragement and assistance; Professor Emeritus Paul J. Wuest for his generously offered expertise; Tony Sanfilippo for his patient guidance and support; Laura Reed-Morrisson, Patty Mitchell, and Michael B. Richards for their sharp eyes and pencils; Hollis Zelinsky for her keen perceptions; and my father, William D. Russell, for buying me a mushroom guidebook when I was a child.

What is a mushroom? Your answer depends on who you are, where you come from, and what you think about mushrooms. For Americans, the white button mushroom *(Agaricus bisporus)* of the supermarkets likely pops to mind. After all, it was the mushroom of our cookbook recipes and restaurant menus before the supermarkets carried a selection of gourmet mushrooms. To people of certain other countries, a mushroom is any edible fungus. Authors of most mushroom field guides apparently use a definition I learned a long time ago: a mushroom is simply "a large fleshy fungus." Defining a mushroom this way opens the door to a broad range of fungi, some with distinctly strange features.

In many ways, fungi are peculiar living things. They have certain characteristics of plants and animals, but they are neither. They have their own biological niche. Botanically, fungi are classed as a kingdom, alongside the plant kingdom and animal kingdom. This distinction indicates the vast differences between fungi and other living things.

Most plants contain chlorophyll, the green coloring matter that uses sunlight to make the sugars that the plant uses for energy. Mushrooms and other fungi, by comparison, don't depend upon sunlight for an energy source, so they don't contain chlorophyll or other such chemicals. (Many mushrooms have green coloring, but not from chlorophyll.) Instead of using sunlight, fungi, including mushrooms, have developed clever ways to make a living. Many are saprophytes: they get their food and energy from digesting dead organic matter. Some are parasitic and draw their nourishment from other living things. Others have a mycorrhizal relationship with other plants, which means that they survive only through a biological companionship with them.

Mushrooms and other fungi play an important role in the balance of nature. They are natural recyclers, helping dispose of dead organic matter and nourishing the soil. Without fungi, dead vegetation would pile up to enormous depths in our forests and elsewhere. The soil would eventually become so depleted of nutrients that green plants could not grow. Without plants, the earth's atmosphere would lose oxygen. Indeed, life couldn't exist without mushrooms and other fungi. (Have you thanked your mushrooms today?)

In other times and places, mushrooms were associated with mysterious creatures of the night, and such folkloric fantasies have not been limited to toads sitting atop toadstools. (How you define a toadstool depends, again, on where you come from geographically. Where I was born, any inedible mushroom is called a toadstool; in other places, people call any mushroom with a cap and a more or less central stem a toadstool. For people with active imaginations, that particular fungal shape is an ideal seat for a toad, should a toad ever be so inclined.) Old and modern fairy-tale books depict pixies, fairies, elves, and other whimsical creatures perching on mushrooms, dancing around them, or loitering in their vicinity. We feel that such creatures are somehow attracted to mushrooms. This old belief probably relates to mushrooms' fast growth—they sometimes pop up almost overnight—and their strange looks. Feeding the fanciful association with little folk, certain mushrooms tend to grow in arcs or circles in pastures, lawns, or other mowed places. In earlier times, these patterns were called "fairy rings," believed to mark the places in which fairies danced. Common names of mushrooms often reflect these quaint beliefs. We still call *Marasmius oreades* the fairy ring mushroom because it tends to grow—you guessed it—in distinct arcs and circles.

Given the right conditions, you can find mushrooms growing almost anywhere and at any time. Woods, lawns, fields, and pastures are their usual habitats. But they can appear in strange places. Although the oyster mushroom (*Pleurotus ostreatus*) prefers dead softwood trees like aspen and elm, it can also grow on the wooden frameworks of houses, weakening the structure by digesting the wood fibers. Honey mushrooms (*Armillaria mellea*) can attack fruit trees with devastating results. Other mushrooms, such as certain *Cordyceps* species, live only on insects.

Some writers include corn smut (*Ustilago maydis*) in their mushroom field guides. You may have seen this common parasite's large, unattractive, sooty black globules on the ears of corn in your vegetable garden. Many feel that including corn smut in a mushroom book pushes the boundaries too far, but it does fit our definition of a mushroom: it is indeed a large, fleshy fungus. Remarkably, it is edible when young, but may be poisonous when it matures and turns black. People of Mexico, the southwest United States, and many other areas consider it a delicacy. In certain places, it is canned and marketed as an expensive gourmet treat. I know no one personally who has eaten it, but I've read comments from people who call it delicious.

A few authors go to the outer limits of the mushroom world and put slime molds in their guidebooks. These peculiar entities aren't true molds, but they are certainly slimy. A slime mold is an organized multicelled mass of jelly-like goo, frequently brightly colored, that slowly creeps along like a giant amoeba, eating dead vegetable matter in its path. It eventually stops moving and develops a spore-producing stage that usually doesn't resemble its former mobile form. Many people find slime molds weird or creepy, but they are interesting to watch and are beautiful in their own way. I've wondered if they inspired those old science fiction catastrophe movies with names like *The Slime That Ate Tokyo.*

Identifying Features

Many wild mushrooms are formed like the white mushrooms of the supermarket. Others look outrageous, even amusing. The yellow morel *(Morchella esculenta)* looks so much like a pinecone that new mushroom hunters often overlook it. The giant puffball *(Langermannia gigantea)* is often mistaken for a soccer ball. *Grifola frondosa,* the hen of the woods, resembles a ruffled chicken!

Certain mushrooms are truly beautiful. The amethyst coral mushroom *(Clavulina amethystina)* resembles purple undersea coral. Earth stars, species of *Geaster,* look much like stars that fell to earth. Certain *Hericium* species resemble miniature frozen waterfalls with cascades of icicles. Mushrooms can indeed look good enough to eat—but beauty is no guide to edibility. Some of the most poisonous species are pretty and even taste good, according to survivors.

Mushrooms display almost any color you can imagine. The golden chanterelle *(Cantharellus cibarius)* radiates a brilliant egg-yolk yellow. Cinnabar chanterelles *(Cantharellus cinnabarinus)* decorate the forest floor with bright orange-pink colors. The bitter-tasting *Tylopilus plumbeoviolaceus* has a violet-gray color, as its scientific name indicates. The parrot mushroom *(Hygrophorus psittacinus)* puts on a spectacular show of rainbow colors.

The tissue of certain mushroom species changes color when you cut or bruise it. *Strobilomyces floccopus,* the old man of the woods, displays white flesh when first cut, but the flesh soon becomes reddish and then later turns black. *Boletus bicolor,* the two-colored bolete, bruises blue. Such color changes are important elements in identification.

When some milky mushrooms (species of *Lactarius*) are cut or broken, they ooze a milky fluid that is often brightly colored. *Lactarius indigo,* the edible and delicious blue milk mushroom, exudes strikingly bright blue milk. The fluid of certain other milky mushrooms changes color when exposed to air. The juice of the yellow milk mushroom *(Lactarius vinaceorufescens)* is white at first, for example, but it quickly turns bright yellow before your eyes.

Other mushrooms glow in the dark, brightening your nightly walk through the woods during warm months. The astringent panus mushroom *(Panellus stypticus)* is a small species that appears abundantly on dead wood. When it grows in vertical columns on a stump, in near darkness, it looks like a miniature skyscraper scene with some of the lights turned on. The inedible but beautiful and well-named jack o' lantern mushroom *(Omphalotus olearius)* forms big orange clusters at the base of dead stumps. Its undersides glow brightly in the dark. Luminescent mushrooms are fascinating. Take them home and put them in the bedroom for an all-night light show. You may have to wait a while, letting your eyes adapt to the dark, before you see the mushrooms glowing. Use them as a ploy to get the kids to hit the sack early.

Mushroom odors are surprising. The edible golden chanterelle *(Cantharellus cibarius)* perfumes a whole room with a rose-apricot scent. Sweet clitocybe *(Clitocybe odora)* smells like anise. Others have peculiar odors. The brown milky mushroom *(Lactarius volemus)* smells fishy after it sits for a while. Eastern matsutake *(Tricholoma caligatum)* can have a distinctly musty aroma. Odors can help you identify a species, but you can't determine edibility from smell alone. Mushrooms with unappealing odors may be good to eat, while others with appetizing smells aren't necessarily edible.

For centuries, Europeans have trained pigs and dogs to find the truffle mushroom, which grows underground and is among the most expensive mushrooms. Finding this fungus would be a hit-or-miss endeavor without the help of the animals' keen noses, and its cost would be astronomical.

Though many edible fungi have a texture like the white button supermarket mushroom, others do not. Shaggy mane mushrooms *(Coprinus comatus),* for example, dissolve into a mush often before you get them home. This process, called autolysis, is the product of an enzyme reaction. The shaggy mane is considered to be a delicacy around the world, but because of its soft, delicate texture, practice and skill are required to handle it properly.

You can't chew or digest the firmest textured mushrooms properly, but you can boil them to extract the flavors. Tough parts of certain polypore mushrooms, such as the black staining polypore *(Meripilus sumstinei),* make a delicious broth that can be the beginning of a fine mushroom soup.

Mushrooms come in a wide range of sizes. The bell-shaped fuzzy foot mushroom *(Xeromphalina campanella)* is the size of a shirt button—so small and delicate that you'll need hours to gather enough for a good meal. Some species, on the other hand, grow too large for one person to carry. Several years ago, my friends and I found a forty-two-pound hen of the woods *(Grifola frondosa).* Unfortunately, it was too old to cut up to eat or preserve. Otherwise, we might still be eating it.

Mushroom Love

Many mushrooms appear almost unearthly, like the imaginings of science fiction writers. Daring thinkers have wondered if they truly originated on earth. They speculate that mushroom spores from distant home planets drifted through space. True aliens, some of these spores reached Earth's atmosphere millions of years ago and landed on a suitable nutrient source, grew, reproduced, and thus found another home. It's fun to ponder, but this scenario has had virtually no support from the scientific community until recently. A few scientists now believe that they have found evidence of simple life forms carried here long ago in meteorites. Stay tuned.

On this planet, at least, mushrooms have a strange and wonderful method of reproduction. When mature, they release a huge number of spores, which are microscopic single-celled reproductive units about the size of human blood cells. Wind, rain, animals, and insects spread them over long distances. If a spore is lucky enough to fall upon a suitable nutrient with the proper moisture and the right temperature, it germinates. At first it extends a finger- or rootlike projection called a *germ tube,* or *hypha,* that quickly grows and branches out into a weak cottony mass, the *hyphae.* Hyphae that grow from a single spore contain only half the genetic material necessary to reproduce the mushroom species. If hyphae of two compatible (yes, mushrooms have compatibility issues, just as we do) spores of the same species find each other, magic happens. As the music swells, they merge to form a hypha whose cells contain the combined genetic material of both parents. Sexual union is now established and the new hyphal tissue is called *mycelium.* This ordinarily invisible, cotton-like fungal mass grows quickly, expands, and eventually gives rise to the mushrooms we pick and put in our baskets.

Mycelial masses can be quite extensive, invading large logs and stumps or covering vast underground areas up to hundreds of feet in all directions. For most mushroom species, the mycelium is white, but for others it is brightly colored. The blewit *(Clitocybe nuda)* has beautiful purple mycelium. The mycelium of the honey mushroom *(Armillaria mellea)* is luminescent. If you have spent much time in the woods on warm summer nights, you have probably seen "foxfire," rotten wood infected by this fungus, glowing with a soft, eerie green light.

Over the centuries, mostly through trial and error and with a good dose of insight, people around the world have learned to harness fungal libido and developed ways to cultivate mushrooms. These techniques have expanded into a worldwide business today. Pennsylvania is the leading commercial producer of mushrooms in the United States, itself one of the largest producers of mushrooms in the world. (On a smaller scale, kits for home mushroom gardens are widely available. Check the Internet for suppliers.) And people everywhere in this country are "discovering" mushrooms. We have never before had such a wide selection of mushrooms available in gourmet food shops and grocery stores; restaurant menus list a variety of fascinating wild mushroom dishes. People are buying mushroom guidebooks and recipe books, joining mushroom clubs, and looking for mushroom training classes, workshops, and walks.

What are mushrooms? They are many things to many people: objects of mystery and fascination, gourmet delicacies, natural recyclers, bases of income, and much more. To those who study and admire them, they are a lifelong source of exploration and adventure.

Collecting and Identifying Mushrooms

Perhaps you have found a colony of delectable-looking mushrooms growing in your backyard recently. Or perhaps you are unfamiliar with mushrooms but would like to know about these backyard visitors. You want to know their names and whether they are good to eat. (Perhaps they inspired you to pick up this book.)

Before we go any further, let me define some frequently used terms in this book. A *mushroomer* is a person who is interested in mushrooms—mainly from a hobbyist's point of view. Many mushroom guidebooks call this kind of person a *mycophile* (that is, a mushroom lover). On the other hand, a *mycologist* is a mushroom scientist, often a college or university professor. *Mushrooming* refers to the varied activities of mushroomers. Some simply want to learn the names of mushrooms they find; others engage in mushroom photography, painting, or drawing; still others study mushroom cultivation. Most mushroomers hope to learn how to recognize edible species and prepare them for the table.

In the following pages, I will often refer to *this region,* meaning the general geographic area covered by the book. When I use the word *local,* I specifically mean the central part of this region, an area around the middle of Pennsylvania. (My turf.)

First Steps

When you find a mushroom, notice how, where, and when it is growing. Certain species prefer to grow singly or in sparse groups, while other species tend to grow in larger numbers, in clusters, groups, circles, and other arrangements. Many grow in woods. Some prefer lawns, pastures, and other places. Notice what the mushroom is growing on: live or dead wood, garden compost, leaf litter, soil, and so on. What season of the year is it? Any information you can get before you collect the mushroom will be helpful in figuring out what it is.

The northeastern United States and mid-Atlantic region

When you collect mushrooms for identification, you will need several specimens in various stages of development. Be sure to cut the mushrooms well below the base of the stem, because important identifying features may lie at the bottom of the stem or even concealed beneath the ground. Don't let the mushrooms you collect sit around too long. Fresh mushrooms are easier to identify than old ones.

Before you put the mushrooms in your collecting basket, smell a couple of specimens to see if you can detect an odor. After the sniff test, cut them lengthwise through the cap and stem. Sniff again. Notice the color of the cut flesh. Watch for a minute to see whether the cut flesh changes color from exposure to the air. Do these tests right away, because they may work only with fresh specimens. You may cautiously want to touch your tongue to the cut mushroom tissue for a brief taste test. No mushroom is so poisonous that a slight touch of your tongue will hurt you. Several mushroom species have an excruciatingly hot taste, however. When you touch your tongue, even briefly, to one of these peppery mushrooms, you won't forget it. (Read more about these hot-tasting species in the section of this volume on edible and non-edible mushrooms.) All of these immediate outdoor tests will help you when you sit down later to identify the species you have collected. Often, mushroomers carry a notebook on their collecting trips to record their on-the-spot observations.

Parts of a Mushroom

To identify mushrooms, we need to know details of the parts that make up their structure. Mushrooms come in a great variety of forms, but to keep things simple, let's begin by examining the common supermarket white button mushroom. The white buttons we buy are the immature stage of a mushroom species that scientists have named *Agaricus bisporus*. As they mature, they lose their button look and develop distinct stems and caps. This is a good one to start with because most people are familiar with it, and many wild mushroom species have a similar form.

The *cap* is usually the first thing we see when we find a mushroom. Because the caps of the various mushroom species can appear vastly different from each other, they help with identification. For example, you can find species with caps whose surface may be smooth, slimy, sticky, scaly, covered with warts, or with a combination of features. Cap colors run the range of the rainbow. The white button mushroom has, obviously, a white cap. Most mushroom books refer to the cap by its scientific name, *pileus* (pronounced PILL-e-us).

The details of the mushroom's *stem,* too, are important in identification. One thing to look for is the position of the stem. Is it more or less *central,* or positioned in or near the middle of the cap, as it is for the white button mushroom? Is it *eccentric,* or off-center? Is it *lateral*—that is, at the edge of the cap? Often you will find mushrooms that lack a stem and are attached to a log or stump by the edge of their caps. In this case, the stem is *absent* or *sessile*. Guidebooks often refer to the stem as the *stipe* or *stalk.*

Aside from the position, many other aspects of the stem—such as the texture, color, and other surface details—are important to notice. What does the bottom of the stem look like (even that part that is buried in the ground)? What about the interior appearance of the stem? Sliced lengthwise, it can show a *solid, pithy,* or *hollow* inside.

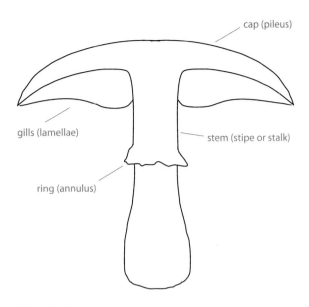

cap (pileus)

gills (lamellae)

stem (stipe or stalk)

ring (annulus)

The parts of a mushroom

Does the stem have a ring? A ring is the remnant of a *veil,* a membrane that extended from the edge of the cap to the stem when the mushroom was immature. As the cap matures, the veil tears, and part may be left on the stem as encircling tissue. Veil remnants may remain on the top or edge of the cap and at the base of the stem, too. White button mushroom stems have distinct rings. The scientific name for a mushroom's stem ring is *annulus* (pronounced ANN-you-lus).

Gills line the underside of the white button mushroom's cap. These are the narrow parallel plates that radiate outward from the stem. In identifying a mushroom species, it's important to note such features as the color, relative spacing, and breadth of the gills. Notice, too, what the gills do near the stem of the mushroom. Are they free from the stem? Do they contact the stem but remain unattached? Are they attached to the stem? If so, do they form a notch or indentation near the stem attachment? For the white button mushroom, the gills are free from the stem; they are a pale pink color when the mushroom is young and become chocolate brown with age. The scientific name for gills is *lamellae* (pronounced la-MELL-ee).

Mushroom gills produce spores on their surfaces. As noted above, spores are tiny one-celled reproductive units, and a single mushroom can produce millions of them. Spores of the various mushroom

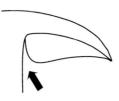

free gills (gills do not contact the stem)

notched gills (gills show a distinct indentation near the stem)

decurrent gills (gills are attached to the stem and run down it)

adnext gills (gills are attached narrowly to the stem)

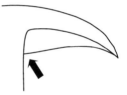

adnate gills (gills are attached broadly to the stem)

The various ways in which the gills meet the stem

species come in a wide range of colors and aid in identification. While the colors of the cap and other parts of a mushroom species can vary as a result of environmental influences, the spore color is much more stable. (You'll need a good microscope to see the spores well, though.) Air currents carry them over great distances because they are so lightweight. If they land in the right place, they will have the food, moisture, and temperature they need to germinate and grow. If all works out well, new offspring of the parent mushroom will be born.

Many mushrooms described in this book lack gills. Some look particularly strange. Puffballs, for example, can resemble golf balls, baseballs, and even soccer

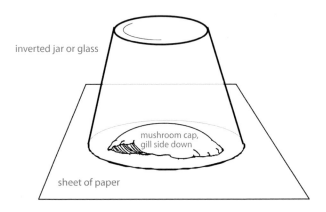

Making a mushroom spore print

Example of a spore print

balls. Spores form inside these round structures. Morels form spores on the wrinkled netlike surface of the cap. Others have many tiny spore-bearing tooth-like projections. This book also includes a number of mushrooms that develop spores inside a layer of pores, which are densely packed, open, hollow tubes.

A look through any guidebook will show you that mushroom species have one or more distinctive features. It pays to learn how to examine the specimens you collect in minute detail, because these distinctions are critical to correctly identifying a mushroom.

The Spore Print

In order to use this or any mushroom book to identify your specimens, you will need to know the color of the spores, especially for gilled mushrooms. You can only be sure of the spore color by collecting a mass of them and looking at them in good daylight. An easy and fun way to do this is to make a *spore print*.

First, cut off the mushroom's stem just below the gills. Next, lay the mushroom cap, gill side down, on a piece of clean paper. Now cover the cap with an inverted jar or bowl to keep the air currents from disturbing the spores that will be released. After a couple of hours, lift off the cover and carefully remove the mushroom cap. You will see a beautiful radiating gill pattern printed on the paper by the mushroom's fallen spores. Note the color. If you make a spore print from a white button mushroom, the color will be chocolate brown. Spore prints are fragile. If you want to keep them, mist them with hair spray. After that, you can put them in an album, if you like.

If you don't see a spore print, or if you get a weak one, perhaps you didn't wait long enough for a sufficient spore fall, or perhaps the mushroom was too old and released its spores before you set it out to print. Sometimes, too, it is difficult to distinguish the spore color from the background color of the paper. To avoid this problem, knowledgeable mushroomers make spore prints on a two-toned sheet of paper: one half of the sheet is white, and the other half, black.

Making a spore print from mushrooms without a spore-bearing surface under the cap can be a challenge. First, you have to determine what part of the mushroom produces the spores. Then you have to find a way to position it over the paper in a way that permits a spore deposit. Sometimes a support, such as a screen or pin, is necessary.

Gathering Mushrooms

Because mushrooms tend to be fragile, it's best to avoid picking them with your bare hands if you can avoid it. Fingernails don't work well. If you try to gather them in this barbaric style you can end up with a basket of unattractive, torn, broken, abbreviated, smashed specimens. With mushrooms in that condition, identification can be difficult. Besides, crushed mushrooms look unappetizing, and you can waste edible parts of the mushrooms if your fingers can't reach the bottom of the stem. So you'll need a good knife for decent collecting. It doesn't have to be a big knife, but the blade should be at least three inches long. I prefer to use a sturdy pocketknife. Many mushroomers keep a large knife in their collecting basket so that it's always on hand for collecting. The knife doesn't have to be extremely sharp, because most mushrooms are easy to cut. For really tough and woody species, such as the artist's conk *(Ganoderma applanatum),* you will need a more aggressive tool. If you are determined to collect this kind of mushroom, you'd better get serious about it and carry an ax.

Mushroomers are particular about their collecting baskets. Most prefer a flat-bottomed basket with a handle. I know mushroomers who use beautiful wide, flat handwoven baskets made of wicker, reed, and other traditional materials. Frequently, these baskets are quite old and have been handed down in the family for generations. Between mushroom hunts, they are carefully stored in a safe place. I like to use an old-fashioned slatted tomato basket made of thin wood. It will last a long time if no one mistakes it for a chair. You can still find these around, but they are rapidly being replaced with cardboard versions. (These modern replacements work just as well, and may even last longer if you remember to keep them out of the rain.)

The mushrooms that you gather in your flat-bottomed basket stay in good condition because they don't crush each other. I like to line the bottom of my basket with a brown paper bag that has been cupped open. You can use newspaper instead. Black-and-white printed pages are the best to use because the paper and ink are harmless. Newspaper print, however, can be transferred to certain mushrooms. It can be disconcerting to sit down at the table and read yesterday's weather report from your dinner. Colored pages in modern newspapers are most likely nontoxic, but they may stain the mushrooms with rainbow colors. Avoid using colored pages from other kinds of publications unless you know that the ink is safe. Be careful when using plastic bags to line the bottom of your basket; they can encourage excess moisture to build up and make a mess of your mushrooms. Many plastic bags are printed with inks that contain lead, too, so if you do use plastic, make sure that any printing on the surface of the bag doesn't contact your mushrooms.

If you need a container to carry mushrooms and you don't have a basket, a paper bag will work in a pinch. These can cause the mushrooms to crush each other, but they are better than plastic bags.

Careful mushroomers carry squares of wax paper in their baskets. When they find a mushroom, they immediately wrap it in a piece of the wax paper to keep it clean, separated, and padded. The mushrooms don't crush each other when wrapped in this way. Paper napkins and tissues don't work well for this purpose, though. They can cling to the surface of sticky or moist mushrooms, posing a cleaning problem when you get back home.

Don't take chances. Whatever kind of collecting container you use, be sure to keep the mushrooms you intend to eat well separated from those that you plan to identify. It's a good idea to use separate containers. Don't leave mushrooms unintended for food lying around where people or pets might find and eat them. Animals can be attracted to certain mushrooms. The poisonous fly mushroom (*Amanita muscaria*), for example, is attractive to cats and can be deadly to them, especially as it dries.

You may want to carry a small brush for cleaning your mushrooms before you put them in your basket. Mushrooms tend to pick up debris that's usually easy to brush off while you have them in hand. Soil that gets trapped in the gills can be especially difficult to remove. (Because mushrooms ordinarily grow with the gill side down, you rarely find them with dirty gills until after you mishandle them.) Putting dirty and clean specimens together in your basket will also create cleanup problems. Indeed, cleaning can be so difficult that you may feel like throwing the collection out with the garbage and warming up a pizza for dinner instead. I've found that each minute spent cleaning mushrooms in the outdoors, as soon you pick them, can save up to five minutes at the kitchen sink. Kitchen supply stores often have cute mushroom-shaped cleaning brushes that you will love to carry in your basket and give as gifts to your mushroomer friends who seem to have everything.

Aside from your guidebooks, you may want to pack a snack, a bottle of drinking water, sun-blocking lotion, and bug repellent for your mushroom collecting trips. Take a cloth to clean the mushrooms, especially if you don't have a mushroom brush with you. If you are planning a mushroom picnic in the woods, you'll need a heat source, such as a portable cookstove or charcoal grill. Don't forget the cooking accessories and tableware. I carry a compact emergency mushroom kit in my car's trunk. It consists of a large paper bag or two, a knife, a few kitchen napkins for cleaning, and sheets of newspaper. If I should come upon a crop of edible wild mushrooms, I have the bare essentials to collect them and get them home. (I've used this kit many times.)

If you plan to eat mushrooms you collect, be sure to collect them in unpolluted areas. Certain fungi take up soil contaminates. Because auto exhaust over the years has contaminated the soil near heavily traveled highways, it's wise not to collect within fifty feet of roadway. Avoid picking in areas that have been sprayed with chemicals. As with any food gathered from the outdoors, be careful of contamination from animal waste.

Identifying Your Mushrooms by Name

Most of us don't have access to a full-time mushroom expert, so we have to rely on our guidebooks to identify the species we find. Because no two authorities describe and illustrate mushrooms in exactly the same way, it's important to have a number of guidebooks on hand—so check your local library or bookstore.

Before we can name the mushrooms we find, we need to know something about how fungi are named by the scientists who study them. As with all living things, mushroom species have a two-part scientific name. (When you see this name in writing, it is printed in italics.) The first part of the name, always capitalized, is the genus. A genus represents a group of mushrooms with certain similar characteristics. The second part, the species name, is given to a mushroom that is distinctly different from the other members of its genus. Some species names are capitalized, but most are not. These scientific names are mainly in Latin—the common language of science—to help scientists around the world communicate.

Most mushroom field guides and identification books use the scientific names. People who know the mushrooms that grow around them, though, also use common, or familiar, names. Although most guides also include a number of common mushroom names, this practice can cause confusion. The common name for a mushroom species can vary from place to place. If you want to be accurate in your communications with other mushroomers and to use guidebooks with ease, you will need to become comfortable with scientific names.

The white button mushroom's scientific name is *Agaricus bisporus.* (It's also named *Agaricus brunnescens* in some books.) All mushrooms included in the genus *Agaricus* have a ring on the stem and grow only on the ground or in rich compost. They also have pink or pale gills when young that become dark chocolate or blackish brown colored when mature. In addition, their gills are unattached to the stem and produce chocolate brown colored spores. The species name, *bisporus,* refers to the way in which the spores are produced on the gills. You'll need a good microscope to see this feature. This species has other distinct characteristics that allow it to be identified without the use of extreme magnification. For one thing, it rarely grows in the wild in our area, but you can find it growing in mushroom compost—the rich soil/manure mix used by commercial mushroom cultivators to grow white button mushrooms. When spent and no longer able to support large mushroom crops, it is sold for enriching vegetable and flower garden soil. It often produces small crops of white buttons for a while where it is spread around plantings.

I don't know many mushroomers—even those who can identify hundreds of mushrooms—who own or use a microscope. If you get deeply into the study of mushrooms, you will eventually find that you will need a microscope to distinguish very closely related species. But don't run out and buy one tomorrow. When you decide to get a microscope, be sure to buy a good one. Toy microscopes or most student microscopes simply won't do the job for mushroom identification work. You will need one of laboratory quality that offers about 1000x magnification with an oil immersion lens. New ones can be quite expensive, so consider shopping for a used one. An older model in good condition will do nicely.

If you want to know more about the botanical classification and naming of mushrooms, you will find many books in libraries and bookstores that cover the subject in detail. In this book, we will be mainly concerned with three categories of mushrooms: the gilled, the pored, and a few of those with neither gills nor pores. To use this book to identify the mushrooms that you find, go on to the next section, "One Hundred Mushrooms."

One Hundred Mushrooms

This guide describes one hundred mushrooms that can be found growing in the central Pennsylvania region. These species also commonly grow throughout a large area of the northeastern part of the United States and into southeastern Canada. Here, they are roughly divided into four seasons of growth: spring, March to May; summer, June to August; fall, September to November; and winter, December to February. Under each seasonal section, the mushrooms are further divided into three subcategories:

- gilled mushrooms (with thin parallel bladelike plates lining the underside of the cap);
- pored mushrooms (with a layer of pores, not gills, lining the underside of the cap); and
- mushrooms that are neither gilled nor pored.

Gilled mushrooms are further divided by spore print color: white, pink, brown, purple, and black. See the directions for making spore prints under "Mushroom Basics," and use the closest color match.

Pored mushrooms include boletes and polypores. Boletes are fleshy mushrooms with a more or less central stem and a spongelike layer of pores on the underside of the cap. On boletes, the pore layer usually separates easily from the cap. Polypores, in contrast, are usually wood-growing, tough or woody shelflike mushrooms with a typically off-center stem—or no stem—and a firm layer of pores under the cap. This pore layer does not separate easily from the cap.

Some mushrooms are neither gilled nor pored. Certain chanterelles—a family of trumpet-shaped fleshy mushrooms generally considered to be non-gilled—can display gill-like patterns beneath the cap.

Dividing wild mushrooms into seasons of growth is not as simple as, for example, categorizing wildflowers. Many mushroom species can appear over much longer periods of time and crop up in almost any season, given the right weather conditions. The seasonal categories selected for the mushrooms described in this book are determined by when the mushrooms are likely to be most abundant or most noticeable—or when local mushroomers tend to think of them as a prominent part of the mushroom landscape. So use these seasonal divisions only as beginner's guidelines. If you don't find the mushroom you are trying to identify in a certain seasonal category, check out the other sections.

Use the categories to narrow your search. If you find a photograph that seems to match your mushroom, read the description carefully. If all the details fit, there's a good chance that you have made a successful identification. Experienced mushroomers don't stop there, though. They use as many mushroom identification books as they can locate to check and recheck the photographs and illustrations; they compare other writers' descriptions of the species as well. They may contact a more knowledgeable mushroomer to confirm the identification, or they may get together in a group to discuss the identification of the mushroom species.

Many mushroomers are interested in identification because they want to learn to collect and use edible species. Wise mushroomers do not immediately eat a mushroom species that they have newly identified. They may wait for a couple of years to become more familiar with the species, just to be sure that it is what they think it is. (If you are interested in eating wild mushrooms, see the "Edible and Non-Edible Mushrooms" section of the book.)

Except where noted, the scientific names of the species included in this book are derived from *Mushrooms of Northeastern North America* by Alan E. Bessette, Arleen R. Bessette, and David W. Fischer (New York: Syracuse University Press, 1997). The mycologists' names given after each mushroom's scientific name refer to those people who provided authoritative references for the mushroom and, in some cases, accounted for changes in nomenclature. Along with the mushrooms' scientific names, I include common names. Some are widely recognized; others are simple translations of the scientific names. For certain species, I also include colloquial and ethnic names handed down from immigrant ancestors.

Obscure mushrooms often don't have widely known common, or familiar, names because people have not paid much attention to them. In their attempts to be accessible, mushroom guidebook authors frequently make up their own common names. This may be comforting to beginners, but it is confusing if your mushroomer friends have not read the same guidebooks that you have. So to communicate with everyone, we must use a mushroom's universally recognized scientific name. Novices often feel intimidated about using scientific names because they feel that they are difficult to pronounce. They don't want to feel embarrassed by saying scientific names incorrectly. Precise accuracy in pronunciation is not important, though; being understood is the issue. What matters is that others know exactly what mushroom species you are talking about, no matter how much you mess up the pronunciation. There's no need to feel embarrassed, because most mushroom "experts" will respect you for giving the name a try. Besides, you must become familiar with scientific names to become truly proficient in identifying mushrooms. All the most useful guidebooks and serious mushroomers use them. To help you, I have included phonetic pronunciations for each species in this book.

Except where noted, photos in this book were taken by the author.

spring
mushrooms

1 Scaly inky cap

Coprinus variegatus Peck
(co-PRY-nus va-ree-eh-GAY-tus)

May be the same as *Coprinus quadrifidus.*

Some mushrooms are orphans. We neglect them—perhaps because we don't know much about them, or because they don't look or smell nice. Our guidebooks give them little attention or completely exclude them. We often find them stomped by someone to "save the children" who might otherwise ingest them. Such disdain may be understandable for the countless numbers of anonymous little brown mushroom species of unknown edibility. But to treat *Coprinus variegatus* this way seems downright unfair. It's a large, common, attractive species that grows in conspicuous, dense clusters that can hardly escape anyone's attention.

Perhaps the scorn comes from the mushroom's odor. Some mushroomers have suggested that it smells like a mixture of spoiled garlic and rubber tires. Or perhaps we don't like the mangy appearance of the caps as the grayish skin flakes away, exposing a shiny bald surface. Some of the guidebooks that include the scaly inky cap warn about stomach upsets and advise us to keep it out of the kitchen. Perhaps its reputation is justified, but I know a number of mushroomers who eat this species frequently and enjoy it. Personally, I have eaten it for a long time with no negative side effects. I think it's the best of the inky caps, with a richer flavor and better texture than the famous shaggy mane. (I don't take it home, however, if it smells particularly strong.)

In a nutshell: Large, dense clusters of egg-shaped, grayish mushrooms with flaky, grayish white patches on the caps; white gills that become inky black with age. Grows on rotting hardwood stumps or buried wood.

Cap: ¾" to 2" across; grayish to gray-brown; covered with a thin feltlike skin that breaks up into patches, exposing a shiny cap surface.

Gills: White, becoming purplish, then black. They dissolve into a black paste when old, like those of other inky cap mushrooms.

Spore print: Black.

Stem: 1 ½" to 4 ¾" long, ³/₁₆" to ⅜" thick; white, with brownish rootlike threads at the base.

Growth habit: In large dense clusters on rotting hardwood. June to July.

Edibility: Questionable; it has caused stomach upsets. Be careful, and avoid the bad-smelling kind.

Copycats: Shaggy mane *(Coprinus comatus)* grows on the ground and not in dense clusters. The common inky cap *(C. atramentarius)* does not have a patchy cap and grows on the ground.

Tip: Because of its reputation, I do not recommend that you eat this mushroom. If you choose to experiment, remember its history of causing gastric upset. Perhaps some people are sensitive to it, or perhaps certain varieties are simply inedible. Like *Coprinus atramentarius,* the scaly inky cap has been reported to cause sickness when consumed with alcohol.

---

2 **Wine cap mushroom**

Stropharia rugosoannulata Farlow : Murrill
(stroe-FA-ree-ah roo-go-so-ann-you-LAY-tah)

Known locally as SRA.

After you learn to identify this spectacular and very common burgundy-colored mushroom, you will wonder why so few people know about it. It catches everyone's attention, making them wonder if they can take it home for dinner. Though a tempting appearance is not a guide to edibility in mushrooms, in this case, the wine cap's looks tell the truth: this is a fine edible mushroom.

When you hunt for this mushroom, you will eventually come upon some specimens whose size will amaze you. I have measured mature wine caps more than fourteen inches across, and I have found buttons weighing more than a pound. One of these can feed a whole family. Mushroomers wonder if these giants grow so big because of ideal conditions or because of their genetics. Perhaps both factors are involved.

You will find wine caps growing in lawns and woodsy places, but they are most at home on hardwood-chip piles. Large colonies frequently appear in places landscaped with wood-chip mulch. Don't forget to visit sawmills and check out the debris piles. Often, nurseries that sell shrubs and trees for landscapers use a lot of wood-chip mulch in their operations. Before you collect the mushrooms from these places, it's a good idea to ask whether poisons have been sprayed.

Characteristically, the spore color of *Stropharia* species is black or deep purple-brown. Mature wine cap mushrooms will normally have black gills, colored by the spores. In at least the central part of this region, however, you will often find this species with white gills. You cannot make a spore print from these white-gilled forms because the mushrooms are sterile and do not make spores. I have seen a lot of head scratching when mushroomers try to identify these white-gilled wine caps. Both the sterile and the black-spored forms have the same flavor, but the white form makes more attractive dishes.

> **In a nutshell:**
>
> Big purple-brown caps; purplish black spore print; white stems with a two-layered rough and torn ring. Grows in the spring in wood-chip mulch.

Cap: 1 ½" to 15" across; shiny; with the color of burgundy wine, white, tan, gray, or yellow; smooth, but may develop cracks in old age.

Gills: Attached to the stem; sometimes notched at the stem; white, becoming gray and finally black with age. The sterile, sporeless form's gills remain white.

Spore print: Black to very dark purplish. No spore print for the white-gilled, sterile form.

Stem: 2 ½" to 10" long, ½" to 3" thick; solid and thick; white, discoloring in old age; with a thick, two-layered cottony ring that is grooved like a wagon wheel on top and split and ragged along the edge; with white mycelium strings at the base when you dig it up.

Growth habit: In groups and clusters, often in large quantities, mainly in hardwood-chip mulch but sometimes in woods, straw, gardens, and lawns. From May to October—but in this region, you'll find many more in the spring.

Edibility: Excellent.

Copycats: Not easily confused with other species if you pay attention to the dark reddish cap, the peculiar ragged stem ring, and the black to purple-black spore print. Don't be fooled by the sterile white-gilled form. *Agaricus* species' gills are not attached to the stem, and they give chocolate brown spore prints.

Tip: Wine caps are easy to transplant and grow in your backyard. When you find the mushrooms growing, gather a bucket of wood chips and debris from under and around the growing specimens. As soon as you can (but within a couple of days), mix this material into a large pile of damp, fresh hardwood chips outdoors. If the weather is dry, water the pile occasionally to keep it moist, but avoid overwatering. Rainwater, deionized water, or distilled water is best to use. Don't use hard water, because it contains minerals that can discourage growth. If you use soft tap water, allow it to sit in an open container for a day to dissipate the chlorine. After a month, spread the chip pile out into a bed about six inches deep. If you are successful, you can expect to harvest multiple crops of mushrooms annually for several years, sometimes beginning in the same year that you prepared the bed. If you add fresh hardwood chips every year or two, the bed will produce bountiful crops for many years.

Gilled; brown spores

3 **Cracked agrocybe**
Agrocybe dura (Fries) Singer
(ag-ROSS-sye-bee DUR-rah)

Some authorities have called this species *Agrocybe molesta*, *Pholiota vermiflua*, and *Pholiota dura*.

In this region, *Agrocybe dura* catches everyone's eye because it can appear in large numbers, often around the home, in the spring when few other mushrooms grow. After warm rains from May through June, it crops up in almost every yard, garden, and public place that uses wood-chip mulch. It seems to be underfoot everywhere at these times, and mushroomers and non-mushroomers alike may wonder whether those carpets of big, appealing mushrooms are good to eat.

Considering all the attention this mushroom attracts, it's surprising that it's been omitted from many guidebooks. I know many mushroomers who do not know its name. Perhaps it's been pushed aside because of its resemblance to other species that grow in the same places at the same time. Like *A. dura,* these look-alikes have large white to tan or yellowish caps, up to four inches across; dark brown to rusty spores; and gills attached to the stem. But *A. dura* has a special earmark: its cap surface develops distinct cracks and ridges as it ages.

Most authorities have considered this mushroom to be edible, even excellent. Some modern guide-books, however, caution that the edible properties of brown-spored spring mushrooms have not been studied enough. I know mushroomers who eat *A. dura* every spring and enjoy it, however. I've tried it several times with no ill effects, but I do not find the taste particularly exciting.

In a nutshell: Whitish cap becoming brown in the center and developing cracks; brown gills; white stem with a delicate, short-lived ring. Grows in wood chips and lawns in the spring.

Cap: 1 ½" to 3 ½" across; whitish when young, later becoming tan in the center. The surface breaks into cracks as the mushroom ages. Delicate pieces of cottony white material hang along the cap's edge.

Gills: White when young, becoming dark brown with age; attached to the stem.

Spore print: Rusty brown.

Stem: 1 ½" to 4" long, ¼" to ⅝" thick; white; with a delicate, short-lived ring.

Growth habit: Grows in hot, moist weather. Often grows in large numbers close together on the ground, mainly in wood-chip beds, but also in lawns and waste places. May to June.

Edibility: Edible, but some authorities disagree. Others recommend caution. Be careful.

Copycats: Other *Agrocybe* species do not tend to develop the strongly cracked cap surface. Be sure to take a spore print and check the color to avoid confusing it with other look-alikes.

Tip: If you'd like to see mushrooms decorating the wood-chip mulch patches around the landscaping in your yard, you can easily start your own crops. Simply transplant a handful of chips from a neighbor's mulch patch that hosts a colony of this *Agrocybe* species.

---

4 **Glistening inky cap**
Coprinus micaceus (Bulliard: Fries) Fries
(co-PRY-nus my-CAY-see-us)

Known locally as inky.

I have a deep affection for the inky. It's the first wild mushroom I learned by myself to eat when I was a mycologically precocious youngster. The big patch that grew in my backyard from early spring to fall, year after year, gave me plenty of opportunity to study it carefully. One day, when I could no longer ignore its appeal, I sautéed a small piece. The melt-in-your-mouth tenderness and delicious flavor were unlike anything I had eaten before. To this day, it's one of my favorite edible wild mushrooms.

In this area, the inky is the first good edible wild mushroom species to appear in the spring, before the morels. The first few warm, rainy days in early April bring on large clumps and patches of glistening inky caps. Like the other inky cap species, this one also digests itself quickly. Inkys just don't last long where they grow—or in your basket after you gather them. Get them home quickly and cook them right away, or you will have a pan of black goo. It will still be edible, but not very attractive.

The name "glistening inky cap" refers to the appearance of tiny scales that cover the fresh caps of the mushroom. These scales seem to sparkle and glisten in the sunlight, if you stretch your imagination. The glittery scales help a beginner identify the mushroom, but they usually come off during the first rain or after a day or two of growth.

Inkys grow everywhere around old stumps and in buried rotting wood in warm, wet weather, so they should be easy to cultivate. Nevertheless, you will not see them for sale in the supermarket because of their speedy self-digestion. To enjoy this delicacy, you must learn to identify it and collect it yourself. The mushroom's long growing season, from early spring into late fall, is a bonus for mushroom hunters.

> **In a nutshell:**
>
> Clumps and patches of small tan mushrooms with glistening caps. Grows in suburban areas in lawns and around stumps and trees from early April on.

Cap: ¾" to 2" wide; tan; fragile; bell or egg shaped, closely surrounding the stem when young, then expanding, with lines extending from near the center of the cap to the edge; covered, at first, with small particles that seem to glisten in the sun like little flakes of mica.

Gills: Crowded together; white when young, but becoming black and mushy with age.

Spore print: Dark brown, but it's not easy to make a spore print because the gills liquefy so quickly.

Stem: 1" to 3" long; skinny, hollow, and smooth; fragile.

Growth habit: Very common. Grows in patches and clumps around stumps, at the base of trees, and in grassy areas from buried wood. Prefers suburban areas. Fortunately, it can grow several times a year in the same place. April to October.

Edibility: Excellent.

Copycats: The edible *Coprinus disseminatus* does not dissolve and has a translucent, more delicate, smaller cap.

Tip: This mushroom is so tender that it breaks apart and crumbles when you harvest the clumps with a knife. Scissors work much better.

---

5 ## Mower's mushroom
Panaeolus foenisecii (Persoon : Fries) Kühner
(pa-NAY-oh-lus fay-neh-SEK-key-eye)

Some authors have called this species *Panaeolina foenisecii* and *Psilocybe foenisecii*.

You probably don't realize it, but every time you mow your lawn in the spring and summer you probably behead hundreds of tiny mower's mushrooms. In this part of the country they grow in practically every chemically untreated lawn. Most people don't notice mower's mushrooms because of their small size. Occasionally, a huge crop covers a lawn like a brown blanket—and then they get your attention.

When I was a little boy, an enormous crop appeared on a golf course near my home. Thousands of mower's mushrooms carpeted acres of the fairway. They made the grass so slippery that golfers lost their footing on the sloped areas. Using a leaf rake, I collected many mushrooms by sweeping them into piles. That evening I had a big meal of mower's mushrooms for dinner. (Never again did they grow in such quantities on that golf course; perhaps the people in charge of course maintenance prevented the mushrooms' return by applying chemicals.)

The mushroom books available to me as a youngster described this species as edible. Whenever I found it, I gathered it for dinner because I enjoyed its fine, earthy flavor and delicate texture. Some later books, however, warned that mower's mushrooms sometimes contain traces of psilocybin—the active agent in psychedelic mushrooms. Maybe so, but I have not heard of anyone in this region experiencing any strange effects from eating this species. Either the mower's mushrooms that grow here do not contain psilocybin or they have very low levels of the compound. Otherwise, my unwitting youthful experiences of consuming large quantities of mower's mushrooms would have produced some unexpected effects.

Be careful with your identification. Mower's mushrooms resemble some inedible and some deadly poisonous species.

 In a nutshell: Small mushrooms with brown conical caps that can develop light- and dark-colored bands when drying; dark brown spores; thin, fragile stem without a ring. Grows in grass.

Cap: Only ½" to 1" across; bell shaped; pale when dry, but brown when moist, often showing both colors as bands when partially dry.

Gills: Brown; attached to the stem.

Spore Print: Dark brown.

Stem: 2" to 3" long; skinny, like a toothpick; fragile, brittle, and hollow; pale brownish; no ring.

Growth habit: Very common. Scattered in lawns, not on dung. From spring to fall.

Edibility: Not recommended.

Copycats: *Conocybe* species have cinnamon brown to rusty brown spores, not dark brown. They tend to be more fragile, delicate, and shorter lived than mower's mushrooms. *Conocybe filaris,* the deadly cone head, is extremely poisonous. It has a distinct ring about halfway up the stem. *Coprinus* species (inky caps) soon dissolve themselves and typically have black spores. Other *Panaeolus* species grow mainly on dung and have black spores.

Tip: I don't recommend that you gather this mushroom for any purpose. Tiny amounts of psilocybin can show up in laboratory tests. If the authorities suspect you of collecting "magic mushrooms," you could be in trouble. Picking a single specimen could put you in jail. Often, the police and legal authorities will not accept the explanation that you are collecting mushrooms only for study. Unfortunately, we have to be careful about what we put in our baskets.

Gilled; pink spores

6 **Fawn mushroom, deer mushroom**
Pluteus cervinus (Schaeffer : Fries) Kummer
(PLOO-tee-us ser-VIE-nus)

Also known as *Pluteus atricapillus*.

One of the great mushroom mysteries is why people call this species the fawn or deer mushroom. I've never heard anyone say that it's the favorite food of that animal—or any other animal, for that matter. Besides, the cap color is usually gray to grayish brown, not at all the color of a deer, at least in this region.

Anyway, mycologists long ago decided to honor the folk name by calling it *Pluteus cervinus,* which translates as a "shed-shaped mushroom that resembles a fawn." To stir up more puzzlement, we can ask how a mushroom with a cap and central stem can be described as being shaped like a shed.

Of the many edible mushrooms that grow in this area, this is not one of my favorites. Although I have eaten it several times, I'm not eager to try it again. Practically all mushroom authorities consider it to be edible, and several of them call it excellent. Some writers recommend eating only the young specimens. After you are certain of your identification, you can taste it yourself and make your own decision about the flavor.

> **In a nutshell:**
>
> Very common, handsome, medium-sized grayish brown mushrooms with a white stem; crowded gills, pink with age. Grows on old decaying wood or from underground decaying wood.

The gills of this mushroom tend to make wet splotches on the paper when you make a spore print. Be sure to look for this feature. It will help you learn to identify the species.

Cap: 2" to 2 ½" across; shaped like a bell when young, then expanding; surface smooth or with small hairs that may not be easy to see without a magnifying glass; typically gray-brown colored, but can vary from lighter to darker colors; smells like radishes.

Gills: Deep; not attached to the stem; white when young, but becoming pink from the colored spores with age; crowded; leave wet spots on paper.

Spore print: Pink.

Stem: 2" to 5" long, ¼" to ¾" thick; white; sometimes swollen at the base; separates from the cap easily.

Growth habit: Singly or in groups on rotting wood such as old stumps, logs, and sawdust. May to October.

Edibility: Edible. Some mushroomers like it.

Copycats: Be careful. Poisonous *Entoloma* species grow on the ground and also make pink spore prints. Their gills, however, are attached to the stem. A number of other similar-looking *Pluteus* species could be confused with the deer mushroom, but are probably edible. One of these is the edible *Pluteus magnus,* which has a thicker stem and a darker, wrinkled cap.

Tip: The fawn mushroom likes to grow in old sawdust, so be sure to check debris and waste piles around sawmills.

Gilled; purple spores

7 **Common psathyrella, uncertain hypholoma**
Psathyrella candolleana (Fries) Maire
(sa-thee-RELL-ah can-dole-lee-ANN-ah)

Known locally as uncertains. Older books list this species as *Hypholoma incertum.*

I thought for a while before I decided to include this edible mushroom in this book. The problem is the great number of *Psathyrella* species out there—about four hundred. Mushroomers find many of these difficult to identify. Besides, the common psathyrella resembles some inedible mushrooms not in the *Psathyrella* genus. Yet it is very common, as the name indicates, and some writers consider it one of the best edible mushrooms. It takes advantage of every warm rain that comes along from May to September and comes up in sizeable crops almost overnight. Look for it in the places where you find the glistening inky cap mushroom: lawns, gardens, and around rotting wood.

As mushrooms go, this species is surprisingly fragile. Getting them into your basket intact is difficult. The stems snap from the slightest bend. Their delicate texture gives them a melt-in-your-mouth tenderness when you cook them. You may have to do some experimenting to handle uncertains in appetizing ways, though, because the frail texture offers an interesting challenge to a chef.

This is not a beginner's mushroom. As its older name—uncertain hypholoma—indicates, identification can be a problem. Go slowly with this one. Check out the descriptions, photos, and illustrations in as many books as you can find. They will probably all include this mushroom.

 In a nutshell: Fragile, thin mushroom that fades to white with age; deep purple-brown spores. Grows in groups and patches on lawns and mowed places.

Cap: 1" to 3" across; cone shaped when young; whitish but yellow tinged when moist, especially in the center of the cap; thin and very fragile. Small white fragments of the veil decorate the edge when young.

Gills: Whitish when young, rosy to purplish brown in age; attached to the stem; thin and close together.

Spore print: Deep purple-brown.

Stem: 1" to 3" long; whitish, hollow, and breaks easily.

Growth habit: In patches in lawns, in pastures, by roadsides, and around rotting hardwood stumps. From early May to September.

Edibility: Edible and good, but be sure that you have identified it correctly.

Copycats: Many! Study your guidebooks.

Tip: Make it a goal to learn to identify this mushroom. It can grow in large quantities when few other species are available, and it is very fine flavored. You won't regret the time you put into learning this one.

Gilled; white spores

8 ### Oak-loving collybia
Collybia dryophila (Bulliard: Fries) Kummer
(co-LIB-ee-ah dry-OFF-fih-lah)

Some authorities list it as *Gymnopus dryophila*.

In the deep pine woods and oak forests of this region, the oak-loving collybia grows in beautiful, neat fairy rings in rich loam soil from spring into late fall. You'll frequently find it carpeting shaded places that have been landscaped with chip mulch. In most years, this very common fungus appears as a prominent feature of the mushroom landscape, both here and across the country. Identification is easy when it's infected with collybia jelly, *Syzygospora mycetophila,* because the jelly covers the oak-loving collybia's caps with distinctive pale, gnarled clumps.

In a nutshell:

Thin, brown-capped, brittle, stringy, stemmed mushrooms. Grow in arcs and fairy rings in oak and pine forests and in dense patches on wood chips in shaded places.

Some guidebook authors report that an occasional mushroomer has become ill from eating oak-loving collybias. Yet I (and many other people in this region) eat it regularly with no ill effects. The shady reputation is unfortunate because the mushroom is quite good, with a sweet, nutty flavor. If you decide to try it yourself, however, do it cautiously.

Don't collect the oak-loving collybia for food in heavily populated areas or places that may be contaminated by industrial waste. This mushroom has the peculiar property of taking up and concentrating mercury. Gather it only in clean, wild places.

Cap: 1" to 2" across; brown to reddish brown; thin and becoming flat, with a wavy edge; moist looking in damp weather.

Gills: White to pale yellow; depressed at the stem; crowded together.

Spore print: White to pale cream color.

Stem: 2" to 4" long, ¹⁄₁₆" to ⅛" thick; colored like the cap or paler; smooth; hollow; brittle and stringy.

Growth habit: In arcs and fairy rings in oak and pine woods, and in carpets of clusters on wood-chip mulch. May to October.

Edibility: Edible and fine-flavored, but may make some people ill. Use caution. Don't collect it in contaminated places.

Copycats: The edible fairy ring mushroom, *Marasmius oreades,* prefers open grassy places and has a paler cap. The edible *Collybia butyracea* cap feels like butter and has a pinkish-tinted spore print; the inedible *C. acervata* grows in much tighter, denser clusters and develops a pink gill color with age.

Tip: You can sometimes find the oak-loving collybia when you are hunting for morels.

---

9 **Fairy ring mushroom**
Marasmius oreades (Bolton : Fries) Fries
(ma-RAS-me-us or-ree-AY-dees)

Known locally as fairy rings.

It can take you a while to learn this mushroom because it looks like so many other small brown species. You won't regret the effort, though, because it's one of the tastiest mushrooms you can find. It has a pleasantly firm, chewy texture and a rich, meaty, spicy flavor. From May through the summer and into the fall, it grows abundantly across this region and much of the United States.

This species commonly grow in circles and arcs in lawns and pastures. In older times, people thought that these were places where fairies danced. If you believe in a world in which magic and "little people" are part of the natural scene, that conclusion may be reasonable. If you tend to believe in a world that is explained only through the principles of science, however, then you may be more comfortable thinking that these circular patterns are a product of biochemistry. The choice is yours.

Fortunately, this is a very common mushroom. It probably grows in your own lawn, unless you use chemicals to suppress fungal growth. You may not have noticed the fairy ring mushroom because of its inconspicuous appearance. Once you learn to identify this species, though, you'll find it growing everywhere. The skinny, rubbery stem and spicy fragrance help distinguish it from other lawn mushrooms.

In a nutshell: Pale tan caps with a central knob; shrivels in dry weather; white spores; widely spaced deep gills; thin, tough stems. Grows in arcs and circles in grass.

Cap: 1" to 2" across; smooth, firm, and fleshy, usually with a knob rising in the center of the cap; tan, whitish, and often the color of coffee with lots of cream; shrivels easily in dry weather; pleasant, spicy odor.

Gills: Far apart and deep; attached, touching, or free from the stem, but not extending down the stem; whitish to pale tan.

Spore print: White.

Stem: 1 ½" to 2" long, ¹⁄₁₆" to ¼" thick; tough; can be bent and twisted without breaking; colored like the cap.

Growth habit: In arcs and circles in lawns, parks, cemeteries, golf courses, and grassy places such as pastures, usually in suburban areas. It leaves a darker green coloring to the grass where it grows, marking its location even out of season. May to October.

Edibility: Excellent. Be sure to dry lots of fairy rings for winter use.

Copycats: Be sure that the spore print is white. Other mushrooms can grow in arcs too. Avoid the poisonous "sweater," *Clitocybe dealbata*, which also has white spores. *C. dealbata* grows in grass, sometimes in arcs, but it has no knob on the cap and no spicy odor; its crowded, shallow gills are attached to the stem or run down it.

Tip: If you don't have fairy ring mushrooms growing in your lawn, you may be able to establish a patch easily. When you find a colony, shovel out a clump of sod about six inches deep and about a foot across with the mushrooms. (Be sure to fill the hole with soil so that the next passerby does not step in it and injure an ankle.) When you get home, dig a hole in your lawn and set the clump in. Watch for the fairy ring mushrooms to begin appearing next spring.

Neither gilled nor pored

10 **Collybia jelly**
Syzygospora mycetophila (Peck) Ginns
(sih-zee-GOS-po-ra my-seh-TOFF-fih-lah)

Also called *Christiansenia mycetophila* and *Tremella mycetophila* in some guidebooks.

Be prepared for a mild shock when you first see the strange, large, tan, brainlike globs of collybia jelly decorating the caps of the very common oak-loving collybia mushroom, *Collybia dryophila*. Not long ago, mycologists considered these peculiar jellylike masses to be the fungal bodies of the collybia jelly mushroom. Now they know that they are tumorlike growths of the tissue of oak-loving collybia, stimulated by the presence of the parasitic collybia jelly fungus. Depending upon your orientation, you will see these strange forms as either attractive or creepy. The fungus is scarce in some parts of the country, but you'll frequently find it in this region. In some years here, the jelly infects most colonies of the oak-loving collybia.

Both older and modern authorities differ in their opinions about collybia jelly's edibility. Some take the safe ground and simply say that the edibility is unknown. Don't be too disappointed in its shady reputation, though. Like many jelly mushrooms, collybia jelly has a gooey texture and bland flavor when cooked. You won't miss much by avoiding it.

In a nutshell: Clusters of ¼" to 2" of pale yellow or cream colored, waxy, jellylike, brain-shaped globs or chewing gum–like wads.

Growth habit: Only grows parasitically on *Collybia dryophila*. May to November.

Edibility: Uncertain. I recommend that you avoid it.

Copycats: Nothing else affects the oak-loving collybia that looks like the collybia jelly.

Tip: Finding this parasitic jelly lets you positively identify the oak-loving collybia, because it only affects that particular mushroom as a parasite.

---

11   Morel
Several species of *Morchella*
(mor-KELL-ah)

Known locally as spring mushroom.

No other mushroom can put so many couch potatoes in the woods as the morel. Like the annual migration of lemmings to the sea, morels can motivate even the most dedicated sofa surfer to set aside the TV remote and head for the forest in the spring. Maybe the urge has to do with the rising of sap in the trees, the annual revival of life, or some elemental hormonal stirrings. For whatever reason, you'll find the most unlikely people searching the woods, hoping to beat other mushroomers to their favorite fungus.

In a nutshell:

All morel species have a hollow cap and stem. The cap, intergrown with the stem, is typically shaped like an upside-down ice cream cone and coarsely honeycombed or netted with pits. The whitish or yellowish stem is wrinkled.

Competition is fierce, and secrecy and deception are part of the sport. I know a mushroomer who wears camouflage clothing and crawls on his belly for hundreds of feet to his secret morel patch. Another piles brush loosely over his plot to hide the developing mushrooms. Beginners, feigning ignorance, soon learn that it's not at all polite to ask a successful hunter where he found all those funny-looking fungi filling his basket.

Recently, a neighbor wearing a sly keeper-of-the-keys grin showed me a big basket of morels. After a good laugh, he proudly announced that he had found them not far from my front door. Big mistake. I located the site and beat him to the mushrooms every year thereafter.

Several places across the country where morels are plentiful sponsor annual festivals, celebrations, and collecting competitions. Mushroomers who find the most morels win prizes. I've wondered whether such heavy harvesting would eventually deplete the morels in these places, but a retired mycologist friend who has attended these affairs for decades tells me that many years of heavy harvesting seem instead to have increased the number of morels. Check the Internet to find morel festivals near you.

Morels are where you find them. I've seen them in such unlikely places as along a street in front of an apartment building and on a barren mountainside. They appear around poplar, pine, cherry, black walnut, wild crabapple, and tulip trees, but they don't grow in these places everywhere. In the central part of this region, you'll most likely find them around old apple trees and dying elm trees. If you want to hunt morels in a certain area, try to discover what kinds of places the local morel hunters explore. (Good luck.)

Besides the challenge of finding a place where morels grow, there is the difficulty of *seeing* them. Although they have a very distinctive look, they also have an amazing ability to be invisible. A beginning mushroomer standing in the middle of a big morel patch can be unaware of the mushrooms' presence until an experienced companion points them out. Morels look like last year's rotting apples, dried leaves, and pinecones. When I was mushroom hunting on a rainy day on a hillside, many of the small wet rocks looked so much like morels that I had to touch them to be sure.

Mushroom authorities worry about just how many different species of morels exist. You can drive yourself crazy trying to pin down the scientific name of every morel you find. Intergradation of the various species' features can cause problems with identification. Some experts feel that there are many different species, but others narrow the genus down to only a few. In your various mushroom books, you'll see that authors often use different names for the same morel species—which really makes things confusing. For the typical weekend morel hunter, such problems don't deserve a second thought. In a stew pot, a morel is a morel. (Just be sure that it's a morel.)

To keep things simple, we'll lump the most common morels into only five species. In order of their appearance in this region, they are the semi-free morel, black morel, yellow morel, big foot, and white morel.

- Semi-free morel *(Morchella semilibera)* De Chambre: Fries. Appears about four weeks before the apple trees bloom; bottom of the cap is not attached to the stem.
- Black morel *(M. elata)* Fries complex. Comes on about two weeks before the apple trees bloom; cap is black.
- Yellow morel *(M. esculenta)* Fries. Look for it when apple trees are in bloom; cap color ranges from yellow-brown to tan.
- Big foot *(M. crassipes)* Fries. Appears just after the apple trees stop blooming; usually colored like the yellow morel, but is grayer when young; can be huge.
- White morel *(M. deliciosa)* Fries. Comes on with big foot morel or slightly later; cap ridges are white when young.

Cap: ¾" to 7" high, ⅜" to 3 ½" wide; tan, black, or with white ridges, depending on the species; shaped like an upside-down ice cream cone, with deep honeycomb or netlike pits or wrinkles; hollow.

Stem: 1" to 5" long, ½" to 3 ¼" thick; white or yellowish; hollow; wrinkled.

Spore print: Cream to light yellow.

Growth habit: Look everywhere on the ground. Try old orchards, around old elm trees, and in burned-over areas. April and May.

Edibility: Excellent.

Copycats: Dangerously poisonous false morels (*Gyromitra* species) vaguely resemble morels. They are easy to tell from morels, though, because they have wrinkled or gnarled caps instead of the coarse honeycomb or netlike patterns of morel caps. *Verpa* species' thimble-like caps are attached only to the top of the stem, but *Morchella* species' caps are intergrown with the stem (except for the semi-free morel, *Morchella semilibera*). Eating *Verpa* species is not recommended.

Tip: In this region, start hunting for morels about a month before the apple trees bloom and expect to find them up to a week or two after blooming ends.

Pored (polypores)

12 White chicken mushroom
Laetiporus cincinnatus (Berkeley and Curtis) Gilbertson
(lay-TIP-por-rus sin-sin-A-tus)

Also named *Laetiporus semialbinus* and *Laetiporus sulphureus* var. *semialbinus*. Known locally as spring chicken.

Several guidebooks call this mushroom rare, and some merely give it a token mention because of its scarceness. In certain areas, however, especially in the central part of this region, it is quite easy to find. That makes the local mushroomers happy because it's as good to eat as its famous close relative, the true chicken mushroom, *Laetiporus sulphureus*. When it comes to dining, it doesn't matter which species you toss into the pot, because both taste remarkably like white chicken meat. They differ mainly in their appearance: the white chicken has white undersides, and the true chicken mushroom shows a bright sulfur yellow color beneath. Remember that these are polypore mushrooms, with a layer of fine pores instead of gills lining the undersides of the caps.

Another difference between these two fungi is the time of growth. White chicken season can start as early as May and continue through the summer months. On the other hand, in this region, the true chicken mushroom comes on later and continues to grow until late fall. In a good season, vegetarian mushroomers can have their chicken and eat it too, throughout the warm part of the year.

Some mushroom guidebooks list the white chicken as a distinct species: *Laetiporus semilabinus*. Others treat it as a variety of the true chicken mushroom and call it *L. sulphureus* var. *semialbinus*. The currently accepted name is *L. cincinnatus*.

In a nutshell: Stacked or overlapping shelflike clusters with bright salmon pink tops and white pored undersides.

Cap: 1 ⅛" to 10" across; pinkish orange color; tough and woody when old.

Pores: White.

Spore print: White.

Stem: None, or simple; colored like the cap.

Growth habit: On dead stumps and logs in overlapping shelf- or fan-like clusters. Spring and summer.

Edibility: Good when young.

Copycats: The tops of the true chicken mushroom, *Laetiporus sulphureus*, are bright orange and bright sulfur yellow beneath. The chicken mushroom typically comes on later in the year than the white chicken mushroom.

Tip: This mushroom, rare in many places, is good to eat for several days if it's kept cool. If it were packaged with cooling gel packs, it could be shipped long distances by overnight delivery. (I've thought about setting up exchanges with mushroomers across the country. This way, we could sample species that are rare or do not grow in our own area, but may be common in other places.)

13 **Dryad saddle**

Polyporus squamosus Hudson : Fries
(po-LIP-por-rus squa-MOE-sus)

Known locally as grouse wings, pheasant wings.

You don't have to come home with an empty basket and a long face after an unsuccessful morel hunt. In this region, you can almost always find dryad saddles in morel picking season. Although they are very easy to identify, most morel hunters don't know that they are edible, so they leave them growing where they find them. Many mushroomers won't eat them because they don't appreciate their peculiar odor and taste.

To a fungus lover, this mushroom has appealing qualities. It's very common in this area and grows in large quantities; moreover, it is easy to clean, easy to identify, and can be huge. Fortunately, you can find the dryad saddles in two seasons here: around the time of the late spring frosts, and then often near the time of early fall frosts. But again, the problem is odor and taste. Some people think that the mushroom smells like cucumbers or watermelon. Others think it has a chemical odor like new car upholstery or paint thinner. I've seen mushroomers nauseated by the raw flavor. Nevertheless, many people collect dryad saddles and enjoy eating them every year. Perhaps it's just a matter of getting used to the flavor or learning the proper preparation. No one should mind your collecting as much of this mushroom as you wish, because it's a parasite on many trees, such as maple, willow, poplar, and especially elm.

Dryad saddles have a tender and delicately crunchy texture when young, but they get tough as they age. When old, they often become saddle shaped. Someone with a powerful imagination long ago thought that they would make good riding saddles for fairies and such creatures. Hence the mushroom's common name, after the old Greek name for a forest nymph.

In a nutshell: Large, typically overlapping clusters of pale yellowish mushrooms with brown scales on the surface of the cap; large whitish pores under the cap; stem black near the base. Grows on elm, mainly, during the morel season in the spring.

Cap: 2 ½" to 12" across, and up to 1 ½" thick; whitish to yellowish color and densely covered with brown scales; tender when young; tough when older.

Pores:	Large; white or yellowish; extending down the stem.
Stem:	½" to 2" long, ⅜ to 1 ⅝" thick; off-center; whitish near the top, dull black closer to the base.
Growth habit:	Singly or in overlapping clusters on living or dead hardwoods, especially elm. Grows in May (through morel season) and again in late fall.
Edibility:	Awful to good, depending on the taster and the collection. Use when young or gather the tender edges of older specimens. Don't eat it raw.
Copycats:	This is a good beginner's mushroom because it is very easy to identify. Not much else looks like it, except the edible, closely related *Polyporus fagicola*, which is smaller and less scaly.
Tip:	You can improve the flavor by leaving the lid off the pan while cooking to let some of the strong odors dissipate into the air.

spring mushrooms

1 Scaly inky cap, *Coprinus variegatus,* p. 24

2 Wine cap mushroom, *Stropharia rugosoannulata,* p. 25

3 Cracked agrocybe, *Agrocybe dura,* p. 27

4 Glistening inky cap, *Coprinus micaceus,* p. 29

5 Mower's mushroom, *Panaeolus foenisecii,* p. 30

6 Fawn mushroom, *Pluteus cervinus,* p. 32

7 Common psathyrella, *Psathyrella candolleana,* p. 34

8 Oak-loving collybia, *Collybia dryophila,* p. 35

9 Fairy ring mushroom, *Marasmius oreades,* p. 37

10 Collybia jelly, *Syzygospora mycetophila,* p. 38

11 Morel, *Morchella esculenta,* p. 39

12 White chicken mushroom, *Laetiporus cincinnatus,* p. 42

13 Dryad saddle, *Polyporus squamosus,* p. 44

summer
mushrooms

14   Weeping psathyrella

Psathyrella velutina (Fries) Singer
(sa-thee-RELL-ah vell-you-TIE-nah)

Depending upon the authors and the ages of your guide-books, you can also find this species listed as *Lacrymaria velutina, Hypholoma velutinus,* and *Psathyrella lacrymabunda.*

From the collection of scientific names that the authorities have given to this mushroom over time, you might think that they can't agree on what to call it—or you may wonder whether they have nothing else to do through the winter months except idle away their time by renaming mushrooms. Neither is so. As knowledge of fungi expands, each name change represents an attempt to find a more suitable and meaningful niche for a mushroom species.

Although the authorities have shuffled and changed the name of the weeping psathyrella, each attempt retains important information about this species' significant features. Because droplets of moisture often appear along the edges of the gills, some of the names include a form of the Latin word *lacryma,* which means "tear." Also from Latin, *velutina* means "velvet" or "fleece," like lamb's wool. In Greek, *Psathyrella* relates to "fragile," and *Hypholoma* means "fringe." Looking over the various names at the top of this page, then, we can piece together the picture: we have a weeping, fragile, fringed mushroom with a velvety or fleecy quality. That description is pretty accurate, as you will see below.

In a nutshell:

Fragile, hairy, brownish caps with thin fringe hanging along the edge; deep brown, spotted gills; hairy stem.

Authorities differ, too, about what to tell us about this mushroom's edibility. A number of guidebooks recommend complete avoidance. Some advise caution because of so many look-alikes. Others simply say that it's edible. Many mushroomers in this region like it; I have eaten it frequently for many years. If we were making mistakes in identification, all of our errors have been edible.

Cap: 2" to 4" across; brownish orange to tan; covered with coarse, hairy scales, with a cottony fringe hanging off the edge.

Gills: Attached to the stem, with a narrow depression at the stem; dirty pale yellow when young, becoming dark brown with age; often with droplets of moisture along the edges.

Spore print: Blackish brown.

Stem: 2" to 4" long, ⅛" to ⅜" thick; hairy; with a vague hairy ring, white above the ring, colored like the cap below; hollow.

Growth habit: Scattered on lawns and grassy places; often numerous. July to October.

Edibility: Edible, but remember that some guidebooks recommend caution because of look-alikes.

Copycats: A number of closely related species require microscope work for identification. *Psathyrella maculata* is smaller with dark fuzzy patches on the cap. *P. rigidipes* is also smaller and is more orange colored.

Tip: With the names of fungi so changeable over time, beginners may wonder how we mushroomers keep our footing on this fungal terra not-so-firma. We go with the flow and quickly learn to live with it.

Gilled; brown spores

15 Horse mushroom
Agaricus arvensis Schaeffer : Secretan
(a-GA-rih-cuss are-VENN-sis)

In older books, known as *Psalliota arvensis*.

I think that this big, bulky species should be called "elephant mushroom," because the name "horse mushroom" really doesn't give an accurate notion of the great size that it can reach. Sometimes you can find buttons almost as large as your fist that then expand into caps more than eight inches across. Once in a while, you'll find some giants as big as a dinner plate. You need a big appetite and a large frying pan to handle one of these monsters.

Horse mushrooms grow in open grassy places, typically in horse pastures, especially in the northern part of this region. In the more southern parts, they prefer the company of living spruce trees. You can easily spot them from a long distance because of their big size and bright white caps. In both situations they can form large fairy rings. Standing inside one of these circles can make you feel very small—and as a mushroomer on the hunt, very happy.

Both this species and the meadow mushroom (*Agaricus campestris*) are close relatives of the supermarket button mushroom. Like the meadow mushroom, the horse mushroom is far better flavored than its supermarket relative. It is also much larger, of course, and has a sweet almond scent. Some mushroom books warn that it has caused stomach upsets for some people. I have never met anyone who had this problem; personally, I have eaten this species almost every year for decades and continue to do so. As good as it is, though, resist the temptation to eat a large quantity at first. Try a small amount to determine whether you are sensitive to the horse mushroom.

As you learn to identify this and other *Agaricus* species, make spore prints. You will need to be sure that you don't confuse this mushroom with the poisonous white species of *Amanita*. Remember, *Amanita* species have white spores; *Agaricus* species have dark brown spores.

In a nutshell: Big white to pale yellow caps, bruising yellow, with a sweet almond scent; a yellow-bruising stem with a prominent ring that shows a star or gear shape underneath when young. Grows in grassy places, often with spruce.

Cap: 2 ½" up to 10" or more across; thick; smooth, but sometimes with a few flakes or scales around the center; white or slightly yellow tinted, often turning yellow where bruised from handling.

Gills: Pale grayish pink, becoming chocolate brown or nearly black when old; free from the stem.

Spore print: Chocolate brown.

Stem: 2" to 5" long, ½" to 2 ¼" thick; hollow; mostly smooth; white, sometimes yellowish, and often bruises yellow; with a heavy ring that has a cottony starlike pattern on the underside.

Growth habit: In grassy places alone, in groups, and in arcs and circles; often around spruce trees. June to October.

Edibility: Excellent, but eat a small amount first to see whether you are prone to stomach upset.

Copycats: The meadow mushroom, *Agaricus campestris*, has pink gills when young, is generally smaller, and does not bruise yellow. Be sure not to confuse horse mushrooms with deadly white *Amanita* species: you will see dark brown spore prints for *Agaricus*, but white spore prints for *Amanita*.

Tip: It's been reported that yellow-staining *Agaricus* species like the horse mushroom can take up lead, mercury, and other heavy metals from the environment. It may be wise not to gather them from treated lawns and near heavily traveled roads. Some mushroomers don't gather any mushroom species within about one hundred feet of a heavily traveled highway. Likewise, some avoid gathering mushrooms that grow in metropolitan areas.

---

16 **Meadow mushroom, field mushroom, pasture mushroom**
Agaricus campestris Linnaeus : Fries
(a-GA-rih-cuss cam-PESS-tris)

Known locally as pink under, pink lady; in older books, *Psalliota campestris*.

When I was a child, lots of meadow mushrooms grew in fields and pastures, where farm animals roamed, and on the fairways of golf courses in this region. Over the years, they seem to have almost disappeared from these places. You can still find them growing, however, in untreated lawns and wild grassy areas. (I can understand why golf course groundskeepers would want to eliminate all of those bewildering golf ball look-alikes, even though the plump white mushroom buttons might provide swing practice for golfers.) Local friends who give their horses and sheep chemical-free, organically grown feed pick lots of meadow mushrooms in their fields.

If you enjoy the supermarket white button mushroom, you will love eating meadow mushrooms. Although these two species of the *Agaricus* genus are related, they are miles apart in flavor. Pasture mushrooms have a tenderness and a rich flavor and aroma that surpass those of their supermarket brothers. Use them in the same recipes as white buttons, and you will be delighted with the results.

When the seasonal conditions and place are good for the growth of meadow mushrooms, you won't have any trouble finding them. The bright white caps are easy to spot against the green background of lawns and mowed places, even from a fast-moving car. As a beginner, when you gather the mushrooms, be sure to turn them over and check to be sure that the young ones have pink-colored gills.

> **In a nutshell:**
>
> Bright white, sometimes brownish, smooth caps that, when young, are button shaped; with pink gills. Grows in grass.

Cap: 1 ½" to 3" across; white, sometimes brownish; button shaped when young, flatter in age.

Gills: Delicate pink when young, becoming brown and then black with age; free from the stem.

Spore print: Chocolate brown.

Stem: 2" to 3" long, ⅜" to 1" thick; smooth and white; solid; with a ring, at least when young.

Growth habit: Grassy places, but not in woods. July into September.

Edibility: Excellent. As with all *Agaricus* species, test yourself for sensitivity by trying a small amount the first time you eat it.

Copycats: Be careful when identifying species of *Agaricus*, because they can be hard to distinguish. Compared to the meadow mushroom, the edible horse mushroom (*Agaricus arvensis*) is bigger and bulkier, has a coarser ring on a hollow stem, and pale gills when young. The smooth lepiota (*Lepiota naucinoides*), with white spores and gills, grows with meadow mushrooms in the same places in the fall and can look very much like the meadow mushroom from the top. Poisonous white-capped *Amanita* species also have white gills and white spores. Remember, *Agaricus* species have brown spores.

Tip: If you see various mushroom species growing in your lawn throughout the year, then it is probably healthy enough to grow field mushrooms. Scatter the kitchen trimmings from your meadow mushrooms around the lawn. The spores may find a home there and give rise to a backyard mushroom garden, where mushrooms may appear for many seasons.

---

17   Bracelet cortinarius, bracelet mushroom
Cortinarius armillatus (Fries) Kummer
(cor-tih-NA-ree-us are-mill-LAY-tus)

Of all the gilled mushroom genera, *Cortinarius* has the largest number of species. The bracelet cortinarius is appropriately named, because up to several conspicuous dull reddish-colored bands encircle its stem. The cinnamon brown cap has a cobwebby underside when young, and the mushroom prefers to grow under birch trees, which can further help you in identification.

Older guidebooks claim that many *Cortinarius* species are edible. The entire genus has lost favor over the years, though. The bracelet cortinarius is widely recognized as a good, even fine, edible mushroom, but many authorities now agree that beginners should not eat this species because of the possibility of mistaken identification. A number of experts go even further and recommend that everyone, even experienced mushroomers, should avoid it. People with weak color vision must be particularly careful because they may not be able to see the red bracelets on this mushroom's stem clearly. That could result in a serious misidentification; some other species of *Cortinarius* are dangerously poisonous, and others resemble poisonous mushrooms from other genera.

 In a nutshell: A cinnamon brown mushroom with red bands on the stem. Grows on the ground around birch trees.

Cap: 2" to 5" across; light to dark cinnamon color; smooth, but sometimes covered with fine scales in age; sometimes smells like radish. The underside displays a white cobwebby veil as the young cap expands.

Gills: Partly attached to the stem and often with a notch or depression at the stem; pale cinnamon color when young, becoming dark rusty colored with age.

Spore print: Rusty brown.

Stem: Up to 6" long, about ¾" thick; club shaped; with one or more red bracelets circling the stem.

Growth habit: Scattered on the ground in the woods, especially around birch trees. August to October.

Edibility: Edible, but be extremely careful. Definitely not recommended.

Copycats: Other *Cortinarius* species, some poisonous, may have colored bands on the stem. The deadly poisonous *Cortinarius gentilis* may have yellowish zones on the stem. It is a smaller mushroom with a dark orange-brown cap and prefers to grow under conifer trees. Deadly *C. orellanus*, often with reddish orange bands on the stem, is also smaller and does not have a club-shaped stem. *Hebeloma* and *Inocybe* species tend not to have the strong rusty spore colors of *Cortinarius*. Both of these genera contain many poisonous species.

Tip: Do not be disappointed if you can't find the full name of the *Cortinarius* mushroom that you bring home for study. They can be very difficult to identify. Indeed, some have not yet been authoritatively identified, so you will not find these described in any book.

---

18 Sticky violet cort
Cortinarius iodes Berkeley and Curtis
(cor-tih-NA-ree-us eye-OH-des)

A garish display of bright purple gills when young, a grayish cinnamon-colored spore print, and a slimy purple cap that develops yellow polka dots and streaks—what more could you ask for to make a mushroom easier to identify? *Cortinarius* is a whopper-size genus, with more than one thousand species. It is notoriously difficult to navigate for mushroomers hoping to identify every species that they come across. Once in while, though, nature tosses us a bone. It kindly offers up a no-brainer like the sticky violet cort, which even a rank beginner can recognize. We can thank the old-time mycologists for its unusually brief species name—*iodes*. It's easy to remember, and everyone can pronounce it.

Don't rush out to the woods with your collecting basket when I tell you that this is an edible mushroom. For one thing, no one seems to think highly of the flavor. And if you look through the guidebooks, you get the sense that the authorities are not comfortable about recommending that anyone eat this species. Their comments range from simply "edible" through a cautious "not recommended" to a blanket "avoid all *Cortinarius* species," even though the mushroom has a long history of being collected for the table.

The gill color can change rather quickly from violet to grayish cinnamon as the mushroom ages, so collect specimens in various stages of development for identification. Be sure to make a spore print, too; some small purple-capped species that do not have rusty-colored spores are poisonous.

 In a nutshell: Small, slimy, purple caps with orange-yellow dots and streaks; gills purple and becoming grayish cinnamon–colored with age; rusty-colored spore print.

Cap: 1" to 2" across; slimy and purple colored with yellowish dots, streaks, and splotches; often yellowish at the center.

Gills: Attached to the stem; purple when young, becoming grayish cinnamon with age.

Spore print: Rusty.

Stem: 2" to 3" long, ¼" to ⅜" thick; purplish; slimy; with a thin ring.

Growth habit: Scattered on the ground under deciduous trees. July to September.

Edibility: Not recommended.

Copycats: Poisonous *Inocybe lilacina* and *I. violacea* do not have slimy caps and make brown spore prints, not rusty-colored ones. The inedible *Cortinarius iodioides* has a bitter-tasting, slimy cap surface.

Tip: The easiest way to distinguish *Cortinarius iodes* from *C. iodioides* is to touch your tongue to the cap. *C. iodioides* tastes bitter.

Gilled; pink spores

19 Aborted entoloma

Entoloma abortivum (Berkeley and Curtis) Donk
(en-toe-LOE-ma a-bor-TIE-vum)

Older books list it as *Clitopilus abortivus.* Known locally as mothers and grays.

Practically all guidebooks offer the same warning to mushroomers who wonder about eating *Entoloma* species: don't fool around with them. They are hard to tell apart, and several are poisonous. But almost all mushroom authorities make an exception for the aborted entoloma. Not only is it very easy to identify, but it's good to eat, too. In parts of Mexico, you can often see it for sale in street markets.

This species exhibits a very weird, distinctive feature. Alongside the normally shaped mushrooms, you'll often find gnarled deformations that may remind you of pale, pink-tinted, misshapen puffballs. Our invasive old friend, the edible honey mushroom *(Armillaria mellea),* causes these distortions when its mycelium infects the mycelium of *Entoloma abortivum.* These blobby shapes are dead giveaways and make this species easy to identify. At first, you may not feel comfortable about putting such freaky-looking fungal forms in your frying pan, but after a couple of meals you may change your mind.

While most mushroomers rate this mushroom's flavor as excellent, others think that it has a soggy texture and an unappealing taste. Long cooking improves the quality. The appearance of any food can often affect our opinion of its edibility. Could the mere notion of eating an unsightly and deformed mushroom, such as the aborted entoloma, influence our judgment of its taste?

In a nutshell: Grayish brown caps; pink gills that run down the stem; often growing as whitish pink, distorted, globby, rounded forms.

Cap: 2" to 4" across; gray to grayish brown; covered with delicate silky fuzz.

Gills: Whitish to pale gray when young, then becoming salmon colored; usually run down the stem.

Spore print: Salmon pink.

Stem: 1 ½" to 3" long, ¼" to ½" thick; colored like the cap; slightly fuzzy.

Growth habit: In groups and clusters on the ground in woods and open places. August to September.

Edibility: Edible.

Copycats: It resembles a number of poisonous entolomas, but this is the only one that can grow in misshapen, globular, distorted forms.

Tip: To be extra safe, some mushroomers choose to eat only the aborted forms of this *Entoloma* species. Of course, the normal forms are edible, too, but they resemble poisonous species of the genus.

Gilled; white spores

20 Caesar's mushroom

Amanita caesarea (Scopoli : Fries) Greville complex
(a-mah-NEE-tah say-SAR-ree-ah)

Caesar's mushroom has also been called *Amanita hemibapha* and *Amanita umbonata*.

Many guidebooks wisely recommend that you do not eat any *Amanita* mushroom species because a number of them are deadly poisonous. Yet most authors would consider it a crime to tell you not to put Caesar's mushroom on your list of edible species. This mushroom is so special that they make an exception, but they warn you to be *very* careful. After all, how can they advise you to avoid a mushroom that has been praised and prized around the world for thousands of years and was a favorite of Julius Caesar?

Fortunately, for *experienced* mushroomers, Caesar's mushroom is easy to distinguish from other *Amanita* species. A thick, white, skinlike veil covers the young, often egg-shaped mushroom as it emerges from the soil. Soon, the top of the veil tears open as the smooth, rounded bright orange or red cap emerges. After the mushroom matures, it retains the broken white veil like a large thick sack at the base of the stem. The expanded cap is usually brighter in the center, with radial lines that soon develop along its edge. The gills, stem, and the ring on the stem are clearly yellow colored. Against the dull forest soil, Caesar's mushroom is impressive, with its bright colors and large size—up to ten inches across.

The most likely candidate for confusion with Caesar's mushroom is the similarly colored fly mushroom, *Amanita muscaria*. The differences are clear, however. Fly's gills, stem, and ring are white; Caesar's are yellow. Fly's caps are warty, but can be washed smooth by rain. Caesar's are smooth (but may have a thick sheetlike piece or two of white veil tissue adhering). The base of the fly mushroom's stem is bulb shaped and usually scaly, while the base of the stem of Caesar's mushroom has a generally smaller bulb, which is covered by a large, sacklike white cup.

With the historical glorification, you may imagine that this is undoubtedly the most delicious mushroom in the world. (After all, if Julius Caesar—probably a very picky guy—was dippy over it, it must be good, right?) Opinions about its quality vary, however. Some mushroomers absolutely adore its flavor; to others, it's mediocre. Maybe those who are passionate about it are hypnotized by its reputation, and those who are not impressed had impossibly high expectations. Its true quality probably lies somewhere in the middle. You'll have to decide for yourself someday when you really know your *Amanita* species.

> **In a nutshell:**
>
> Bright reddish orange cap with lines along the edge; yellow gills; yellow ring on the stem; a thick white cup at the base of the stem.

Cap: 2" to 4 ¾" across; red to yellow-orange; sticky; often with a knob in the center. The edge shows little lines that duplicate the pattern of the gills lying beneath.

Gills: Yellow; not attached to the stem.

Spore print: White.

Stem: Yellowish, with a yellow ring and a thick white cup at the base.

Growth habit: Singly, scattered, or sometimes in fairy rings, on the ground in woods. July to September.

Edibility: Good.

Copycats: *Amanita muscaria* and *A. flavoconia* have warts on the cap, at least when young, and lack the thick white cup at the base of the stem. Both are poisonous. *A. parcivolvata* does not have a ring on the stem nor the thick white cup at the base of the stem. It may be poisonous. *A. frostiana*, not edible, also has warts on the cap. All of these look-alikes have white gills, but Caesar's mushroom has yellow gills.

Tip: This one is definitely not for beginners. I know experienced mushroomers who have not eaten Caesar's mushroom, even after many years of mushroom study. They know that it's important to feel absolutely confident in your own mind before you eat any *Amanita* mushroom. Wisely, they're working on it at their own pace.

---

21 **Fly mushroom, fly poison**
Amanita muscaria (Persoon : Fries) Bertillon
(a-mah-NEE-tah mu-SCA-ree-ah for-MOE-sah)

Even if you don't know the fly mushroom by name, you have seen it in children's books, calendar pictures, and kitchen art. This is the mushroom with the bright red or orange cap covered with big white dots. Recently, I saw fly mushroom coffee cups for sale in a department store. I have ceramic fly mushroom salt and pepper shakers on my dining table. I'll bet that you can find a photo or representation of fly mushrooms in almost any home, if you look hard enough. They are everywhere.

With all the attention, you might expect it to be a popular edible mushroom around the world. Unfortunately, it's not. Fly mushrooms are quite poisonous. They rarely cause death, but they will make you very sick if you eat them. (They are one of those toxic mushrooms that can make you *wish* that you were dead for a couple of days.)

In some places, they are carefully prepared in certain ways and eaten for a psychedelic experience. But the varieties of fly mushrooms that grow in much of this region are not used for that purpose. If they have any mind-altering properties, those are far overshadowed by their poisonous effects. That's what I know from the experiences of daring mushroomers who have tried fly mushrooms in the central part of this region.

In a nutshell: Large, yellow to orange capped with large white warts on the cap; ring on a white stem; scaly bulb at the base of the stem.

Cap: Often shown as bright red, but in our region they are yellow to orange; smooth and dotted with large, white, cottage cheese–like spots.

Gills: White; free from the stem.

Spore print: White.

Stem: White; with a ring and with a scaly bulb at the base.

Growth habit: Scattered on the ground in woods or under trees, sometimes growing in fairy rings around the trunk of a tree. July to October.

Edibility: Not edible! They are poisonous.

Copycats: Amanitas have a number of distinct features. Check the "Edible and Non-Edible Mushrooms" section of this book.

Tip: The name "fly poison" comes from the way in which Europeans use this mushroom to rid their houses of flies. You can try it by placing a cap of the mushroom in a saucer of milk and setting it in an open place. Flies can't resist it. Neither can cats, which are particularly vulnerable to the poison, so be careful to keep it away from kitty—and, of course, from little kids.

---

22 **Blusher**

Amanita rubescens (Persoon : Fries) S. F. Gray
(a-mah-NEE-tah roo-BESS-sens)

Newcomers to mushrooming soon learn that deadly poisonous species of *Amanita* account for the majority of mushroom-related fatalities here and abroad.

Many beginners are surprised to discover that not all *Amanita* species are poisonous—and that some, like the blusher, are quite good to eat. A number of mushroomers who live in my vicinity have sampled this very common mushroom (and I have, too). They do not, however, collect and eat it casually, as they would other edible mushrooms. They are uncomfortable about fooling around with an *Amanita* mushroom, especially one that more or less resembles some of the poisonous species of the genus.

Yet several mushroomers in the southern part of this region have told me that the blusher is one of their favorite mushrooms. They gather it every year for the family dinner table. I know of one southern community where blusher collecting is an annual event with plenty of competition. A friend who lives there told me that people have been collecting it for generations and don't worry much about confusing it with poisonous species. Many mushroomers would shake their heads at this relaxed attitude.

As you examine your guidebooks, you will read conflicting comments about the blusher. Some writers praise its edible qualities; others disagree. You will also find the descriptive details varying from writer to writer. That's mainly because the way this species appears in the western part of the country can be quite different from its appearance in the east. Be sure to determine what part of the country, or the world, your guidebooks highlight.

The name "blusher" derives from the reddish stains that the mushroom slowly develops from bruising and with age. That color change is a stable feature of this otherwise variable species, but certain other *Amanita* species show similar color changes. Another characteristic of the blusher mushroom is the chalky appearance of the dried gills.

> **In a nutshell:**
>
> Reddish brown cap with flaky warts; white stem with a ring and bulb at the base; white gills; entire mushroom slowly bruises and ages reddish.

Cap: Egg shaped when young, becoming flatter with age, with pale, flaky warts; variable cap color, ranging from whitish to reddish or reddish brown and even olive tinged; *slowly* becomes reddish where bruised or broken.

Gills: White, with reddish stains; with a characteristic chalky appearance when dry.

Spore print: White.

Stem: White, with dull reddish stains, especially near the bulb-shaped base; covered with small scales; with a fragile ring.

Growth habit: Very common in hardwood or mixed forests. July to September.

Edibility: Edible—but be EXTREMELY CAREFUL!

Copycats: *Amanita pantherina* often has a band of thin cottony tissue around the top edge of the bulb at the base of the stem; *A. muscaria* has a scalier bulb. Neither stains reddish when bruised. Both are poisonous. *A. brunnescens* bruises reddish brown and typically shows a vertical split in the bulb at the base of the stem. *A. flavorubescens* stains reddish but has a yellow-brown to orange-brown cap with yellowish patches. Both of these may be poisonous.

Tip: I don't recommend that you eat any *Amanita* mushroom species until you consider yourself an expert.

---

23 Grisette
Amanita vaginata (Bulliard : Fries) Vittadini
(a-mah-NEE-tah va-jin-NAY-tah)

Older guidebooks call it *Amanitopsis vaginata* and *Vaginata plumbea.*

Mushrooming offers endless surprises. A novice soon learns that some *Amanita* species lack a ring on the stem. I know—photos, diagrams, and illustrations of the "typical" *Amanita* mushroom emphasize the stem ring. Most *Amanitas* have it, including the most dangerous species of the genus. You won't find ringless *Amanita* species in older guidebooks, because in the past, they were placed in another genus, *Amanitopsis.* Not long ago, mycologists decided that the two genera were too similar to be separated. So they dumped the name *Amanitopsis* and lumped both the ringed and ringless species in the *Amanita* genus.

Mushroom scientists constantly work to make fungal classification more meaningful and useful. Some, called "lumpers," prefer to reduce the number of divisions and group mushrooms under fewer names. Others, called "splitters," are convinced that the more divisions the better, and they create finer and finer distinctions among mushrooms. Guidebooks reflect this name juggling—and a beginner quickly learns that it's just part of the game of mushrooming.

In a nutshell: Grayish caps, with deep lines around the top edge of the cap duplicating the gill pattern; a ringless stem with a white, loose, baglike sleeve at the base.

Cap: 1 ¼" to 4" across; thin. Typically gray to grayish brown, but you can find many different cap colors ranging from white through brown, even to black. Sometimes with white patches; with deep lines along the edge of the cap, duplicating the gill pattern that lies beneath.

Gills: White; may be attached or free from the stem.

Spore print: White.

Stem: 2 ¾" to 6" long, ³⁄₁₆" to ½" thick; white; without a ring; has a loose white sack surrounding the base of the stem and attached only at the base.

Growth habit: Singly or in small groups, on the ground under both conifers and hardwoods. July to September.

Edibility: Edible, but be very careful not to confuse it with deadly poisonous species.

Copycats: The reddish brown to tan-colored tawny grisette, *Amanita fulva*, was once considered to be a variety of *A. vaginata*. It's edible, too.

Tip: Cows enjoy eating this mushroom when they find it, but don't depend on an animal's foraging preferences to determine whether a mushroom is good for people to eat. Animals can have different digestive systems from ours.

---

24 **Destroying angel**
Amanita virosa LaMarck
(a-mah-NEE-tah vih-ROE-sah)

Known locally as angel of death, death angel.

Here is the first rule for anyone who wants to learn about edible mushrooms: LEARN TO IDENTIFY THE

DESTROYING ANGEL AND ITS CLOSE RELATIVES. Around the world, most deaths from eating wild mushrooms result from mistaking deadly amanitas, such as these, for safe mushrooms. Destroying angels are common in this region, but their distinguishing features are easy to learn. (See below.)

Certain species of *Amanita* are edible. Nevertheless, many mushroomers, even those with many years of experience, refuse to eat *Amanita* species in order to avoid any chance of being poisoned. In fact, many avoid any mushroom that even resembles an amanita. These precautions go a long way toward preventing accidental deaths from eating poisonous mushrooms. They are not the last word, though, because a few other mushroom species in other genera are just as poisonous. You can read about these in "Edible and Non-Edible Mushrooms."

> **In a nutshell:**
>
> White, with white gills free from the stem; white spores; stem with a ring and a white cup at the base.

A peculiar feature of the destroying angel is its strange luminous aura, a subtle white glow that draws the eye. Unlike the jack o' lantern mushroom, the destroying angel displays no phosphorescence when you take it into a dark room. Yet in the dark forest, *Amanita virosa* is easily visible from a hundred feet away, with its serene, sinister, angelic radiance.

To learn the features of this deadly group, remember the following description.

Cap: 1 ⅛" to 5 ⅛" across; white, or whitish; smooth; without warts.

Gills: White; free from the stem.

Spore print: White, sometimes becoming yellowish or orangish.

Stem: 2 ⅜" to 8" tall, ¼" to ¾" thick; white; often with a rough, cottony surface; with a white ring and with a cuplike enclosure at the base, sometimes buried underground.

Growth habit: Singly, in groups, and occasionally in fairy rings, in forests. Common. June to November.

Edibility: DEADLY POISONOUS.

Copycats: *Amanita verna* has a smoother stem. *A. bisporigera* is smaller. Both have also been called "destroying angel."

A. phalloides often has a greenish-colored cap. All are deadly poisonous.

Tip: Never put destroying angels in your collecting basket. Simply leave them in nature where you find them growing, away from people and pets.

---

25 Wolf asterophora

Asterophora lycoperdoides (Bulliard) Ditmar
(as-ter-RAH-for-ah lie-coe-per-DOY-dees)

Has also been named *Nyctalis asterophora.*

It may come as a mild shock for a newcomer to the world of fungi to learn that certain mushrooms live only as parasites on other mushrooms. After studying fungi and learning about their wide-ranging appetites—from manure to house timbers, and much between—we come to expect their eccentric diet preferences. We can feel relieved that no mushroom species that I know of grows on humans. (There was one that preyed on humans in an old creepy science fiction movie I saw as a youngster. Fortunately, it wasn't scary enough to unnerve me from learning about mushrooms, but those unsavory fungaloids shuffled around in my night dreams for a time.)

In this region, the wolf asterophora grows in colonies, on *Russula nigricans,* but it can also choose a close relative. The unfortunate host is often reduced to an unidentifiable black mass. Although it's considered uncommon in most places, you can find this parasitic species frequently in this region. According to most authorities, its edibility is unknown, so it's best to avoid it. It's not particularly appealing, anyway, with its often gnarled long stem, thickly powdered brown cap surface, and malformed gills.

In a nutshell: White cap covered thickly with brown powder. Grows in groups on old mushrooms.

Cap: ¼" to ¾" across; white, round, becoming thickly covered with brown powdery spores.

Gills: White; attached to stem; usually distorted and sparse, widely spaced, and thick.

Spore print: White, but usually weak.

Stem: ⅛" to 1 ¼" long, ⅛" to ⅜" thick; white, becoming brown with age; often twisted and gnarled.

Growth habit: Several to many specimens, mainly parasitic on certain *Russula* species that naturally become black when deteriorated. July to November.

Edibility: Unknown.

Copycats: *Asterophora parasitica* does not have a powdery cap. *Collybia tuberosa* and its close relatives have well-formed gills and a potatolike tuber at the base of the stem. Both are parasites on other mushrooms.

Tip: With only two known species of *Asterophora*, you shouldn't have trouble handling the genus.

---

26 **Club foot**

Clitocybe clavipes (Fries) Kummer
(cly-TOSS-sye-bee CLA-vih-pes)

It happens all the time. From some old guidebooks, you learn that the common club foot mushroom is good to eat and easy to identify. Your mouth waters a little and you feel happy about discovering another mushroom to bring home for dinner. Then you pick up a modern publication and find that it's not recommended for eating anymore. Like nudging a ripe puffball, your newfound joy goes up in a puff of smoke as you scratch another entry from your edible mushroom list.

Many modern guidebooks warn of the dangers of confusing the club foot with a number of look-alikes. They also report that you may experience discomforts from drinking alcoholic beverages around the time of eating this mushroom. For most mushroomers, these warnings are enough to discourage collecting it for dinner. Yet, with these warnings in mind, I know many people in this region (including myself) who have eaten club foot mushrooms for decades and had no problems. Perhaps we have not consumed enough of the mushroom in conjunction with alcoholic drinks to trigger an uncomfortable reaction. Or, if we confused it with other species, none of those were even mildly toxic.

Most local mushroomers feel that the precautions about confusing the club foot with a no-no mushroom are overblown. Certain related species here have a stem with a swelling at the base, but they don't have the same shape or coloring as the club foot. Perhaps there are more look-alikes outside this area. In any case, don't ignore the warnings of the authorities; be cautious about eating it.

> **In a nutshell:** Thick, funnel-shaped, gray-brown cap; white gills that run down the stem; club-shaped gray-brown stem.

Cap: 1" to 4" across; gray-brown; smooth; thick, funnel shaped, with a flat or sunken top when mature. It often has a sweet, pleasant fragrance.

Gills: White; run down the stem; often forked.

Spore print: White.

Stem: 1 ¼" to 2 ½" long, ¼" to ⅜" thick at top, up to 1 ⅜" thick at base; club shaped; colored like the cap.

Growth habit: On the ground in groups, clusters, and fairy rings under conifer trees. July to October.

Edibility: Edible, but be careful.

Copycats: *Clitocybe subclavipes* grows under hardwoods, not conifers, is paler in color, and has less of a club-shaped stem. Apparently, it too is edible. The stem of *C. nebularis* can be somewhat swollen at the base. It gives a grayish yellow spore print, however, and has an unpleasant skunky odor. It may cause gastric upset.

Tip: To be safe, until you become familiar with the club foot, check its white spore print under natural light to separate it from the pale grayish yellow spore print of the disagreeably scented *C. nebularis*. Yellowish spore prints can look white in incandescent light.

---

27 Orange-gilled waxy cap

Hygrophorus marginatus Peck
(hye-GRAH-for-us mar-jin-NAY-tus CON-co-lor)

You may see this mushroom named *Hygrocybe marginata* var. *concolor* and *Humidicutis marginata* var. *concolor* in certain guidebooks.

Don't let the name confuse you, because the orange-gilled waxy cap doesn't always have orange gills. The *concolor* variety, described here, has gills colored bright yellow, like the cap. *Hygrophorus marginatus* var. *marginata* is the orange-gilled variety. In parts of this region, the yellow-gilled variety is most common. You can have a rough time identifying certain mushrooms like this one if your guidebooks don't tell you about their possible color variations. To further confuse mushroomers, some modern guidebooks use the genus name *Hygrocybe* for this species. No wonder that beginners may feel inspired to swap their mushroom books for crocheting needles or golf clubs.

In a nutshell:

Small, moist, translucent mushrooms, with orange-yellow to yellow caps that fade when old; waxy yellow gills fade more slowly than the cap. Grows on the ground in woods.

The color interplay of the yellow cap and gills of this mushroom is fascinating. When young, both the cap and gills are brightly colored. With age, the cap fades and becomes paler than the gills. In fact, the persistence of the gill color after the cap has faded is a primary identifying feature of this waxy cap species.

You can't help noticing the brightly colored *Hygrophorus* species that grow through the summer and fall months in this region. Their delicately sculptured waxy look and subtle translucent glow help distinguish them from other mushrooms. If you rub your fingers lightly over their gills, you will notice a waxy feel. Many are edible, including the orange-gilled waxy cap, but opinions of their quality vary.

Cap: ½" to 1 ½" across; dried apricot colored to bright yellow; cone shaped when young, flatter when older; moist.

Gills: Bright yellow; attached to the stem; feel waxy.

Spore print: White.

Stem: 1 ¼" to 2 ¼" long, ³⁄₁₆" to ⁵⁄₁₆" thick; bright yellow; moist.

Growth habit: In small groups or singly, on rich soil in hemlock and mixed woods. August to September.

Edibility: Edible.

Copycats: *Hygrophorus flavescens* has a distinctly slimy cap. *H. chlorophanus* has both a slimy cap and stem.

H. miniatus has a bright red cap that fades to yellow when old. All of these are edible.

Tip: At the risk of pushing your patience beyond the limit, I have to tell you about yet another variety of the orange-gilled waxy cap: *H. marginatus* var. *olivaceus*. It's olive-brown colored in the center of the cap and has orange gills.

---

28 False chanterelle

Hygrophoropsis aurantiaca (Wulfen : Fries) Maire
(hye-grow-for-OP-sis are-ran-TIE-ah-cah)

Also called *Clitocybe aurantiaca* and *Cantharellus aurantiacus* in older books.

Don't believe those guidebooks when they tell you that a beginner can easily distinguish the false chanterelle from the edible and delicious golden chanterelle (*Cantharellus cibarius*). Both mushrooms have forked gills and a similar overall form, but there are significant differences. The false chanterelle is distinctly orange in color and has gills that are knife-edge sharp; the golden chanterelle is commonly described as having a yellow color and blunt-edged gills. You'd think that these gross differences would make separating the two species clear and easy, and most of the time they do. Yet the guidebooks don't always emphasize that the golden chanterelle can sometimes have orange hues, or that you can find it with knife-edged gills as sharp as the false chanterelle's, especially in the east (including this region). These variations easily cause confusion. If both were nontoxic, misidentification wouldn't be a problem. Some authorities call the false chanterelle poisonous, yet others consider it edible. Others are uncertain about its edibility. Mushroomers tend to be very cautious about consuming mushrooms with such a hazy reputation.

These two more or less look-alike mushrooms offer us a good lesson: always check your guidebook descriptions thoroughly. If we study the false chanterelle further, we find that it's a flimsier, softer, more delicate mushroom than the golden chanterelle. The false chanterelle's cap is typically less wavy on the edge and tends to be brownish colored in the center. Finally, it lacks the rose-apricot fragrance of the golden chanterelle. Once you become familiar with the false and golden chanterelles, it's easy to tell them apart. But if you are a beginner and have never seen them, take the time to learn their differences.

In a nutshell: Slightly fuzzy, orange caps with a darker center; sharp-edged, forked orange gills running down the stem.

Cap: 1" to 3" across; finely velvety; orange, often browner at the center.

Gills: Orange; running down the stem; close together; knife-edge sharp and forked.

Spore print: White.

Stem: 1" to 3" long, ⅛" to ½" thick; color of cap; maybe off-center.

Growth habit: On the ground in groups and clusters in humus, often under conifers. July to October.

Edibility: Uncertain.

Copycats: The golden chanterelle makes a pale yellow spore print. The jack o' lantern *(Omphalotus olearius)* does not have forked gills, glows in the dark, and is typically a larger mushroom.

Tip: In incandescent light, it's hard to tell the difference between the pale yellow spore print color of the golden chanterelle and the white spore print of the false chanterelle. Always check spore print colors in daylight for accuracy.

---

29 Common laccaria

Laccaria laccata (Scopoli : Fries) Berkeley and Broome
(la-CA-ree-ah la-CAY-tah)

This mushroom is short on flavor but long on availability. First appearing in early spring and continuing into late fall, it's one of our longest fruiting species. It's not especially particular about where it grows. You can find this unfussy fungus in woods, in grassy areas, around trees, and in barren sandy places. If the weather is unfriendly to mushrooms and you can't find anything else to put in your collecting basket, you can often bring home a handful of common laccarias.

Mushroomers know the difficulties of identifying little brown mushrooms. You can use up many hours laboring over your books trying to pin a name on every small brownish species you bring home. All too often, you will only manage bleary-eyed confusion. Even the experts have trouble with them. Many little brown mushrooms are omitted from the guidebooks, because they have not yet been identified.

Fortunately, the common laccaria is one little brown mushroom that is easy to learn to identify, even though its color, size, and form vary widely. Authorities recognize some of these variations as closely related species. Even with this perplexity, practically all writers have listed this mushroom as edible.

In a nutshell:
Small pinkish tan caps with a depression in the center; widely spaced, slightly waxy-feeling pinkish gills; white spores; a tough stem. Very common.

Cap: ½" to 2" across; pale red to pinkish red when moist, pale rusty to tan when dry; often with a dimple or depression in the center.

Gills: Pale pink; often dusted with white powder as the spores develop.

Spore print: White.

Stem: 1" to 3" long, ⅛" to ¼" thick; colored like the cap; tough and stringy.

Growth habit: Scattered about in all kinds of soil and a wide variety of places. May to October.

Edibility: Edible, but uninteresting.

Copycats: You'll need a microscope to separate all the similar-looking *Laccaria* species. I know many mushroomers who eat *Laccaria laccata* every year, and none gets sick. Few of them own a microscope, so they must be regularly eating some of these look-alikes.

Tip: Use this bland-flavored mushroom to add bulk to a dish, rather than flavor. Include it with other, better-tasting mushrooms.

30 Purple-gilled laccaria

Laccaria ochropurpurea (Berkeley) Peck
(la-CA-ree-ah oh-crow-pur-pur-REE-ah)

Known locally as purple gill.

From a mushroomer's point of view, the purple-gilled laccaria has a number of good points. It's edible, beautiful, easy to identify, grows in large quantities, and can appear when other mushroom species are waiting for better weather conditions.

The bad points? To many mushroomers' taste, this species has almost no flavor. The texture is pleasant enough, but its taste is simply boring. You may find it disconcerting to sit down to a beautiful steaming dish of freshly sautéed purple-gilled laccarias and taste only warm butter.

After this surprise, you will probably feel inclined to scratch it off your edible species list. Not so fast. It has a saving grace: the remarkable ability to absorb the flavor of whatever food you cook along with it. If, for example, you cook it with chicken, you get chicken-flavored mushrooms. Cook it with steak and the mushrooms will taste like steak. So it's worth bringing home, if you have something interesting to toss in the pot with it.

In a nutshell: Large, robust, pale purple-brown mushrooms with widely spaced purple gills. Grows on the ground in open places under oak trees.

Cap: 2" to 4" across; watery-looking and purplish brown when moist, but grayish to pale tan when dry; rounded when young, then becoming flat.

Gills: Pale purple, thick, and spaced far apart; attached to the stem.

Spore print: White, sometimes with a pale purple tinge.

Stem: 1 ¼" to 6" across, ⅜" to ¾" thick.

Growth habit: Singly or in groups on the ground in open and grassy places under hardwood trees, especially oaks. July to September.

Edibility: Edible.

Copycats: Of purple mushrooms with white spore prints, the most likely candidate for confusion is *Laccaria amethystina,* which is a smaller mushroom that is entirely colored purple. *L. trullisata* grows in sandy places. Be sure to take a spore print, because the purple gill resembles a number of non-white-spored mushrooms.

Tip: If you collect a basket of purple gills and little else, break out your secret cache of dried morels. Pick out one morel and revive it in water for a while. Then chop it up and sauté it with the purple gills. The whole dish will taste like morels.

---

31   **Wrinkled milky**
Lactarius corrugis Peck
(lack-TA-ree-us co-ROO-gis)

If we didn't have another mushroom named "old man of the woods," this species would be a good contender. With its dark brown wrinkled cap, it looks like a mushroom well past its prime and knocking at death's door. After one sympathetic glance, novices are likely to walk right on by. Knowledgeable mushroomers know better. Even with its shriveled, weather-beaten appearance, they recognize it as a good edible mushroom. Many in the know think that it's one of the best.

The wrinkled milky is easy to identify, so it's another good beginner's mushroom. Few species have such a distinctly wrinkled cap. Like its smoother-capped and lighter-colored close relative, the orange-brown milky *(Lactarius volemus),* it gushes mild-tasting white milk when it's bruised or broken. Wrinkled milkys tend to be more robust than brown milkys, however. They also have gills of a more tan color and may not gush so much milk. A peculiarity of the wrinkled milky mushroom is the fuzzy appearance of the edge of its gills under a magnifying glass.

 In a nutshell: Dark reddish brown, strongly wrinkled caps; gushes mild-tasting white milk where injured; dark cream- to pale cinnamon-colored gills.

Cap: 3" to 5" across; yellow-brown to dark reddish brown; dry, velvety, and strongly wrinkled. It gushes mild-tasting white milk when cut or broken.

Gills: Dark cream yellow or cinnamon colored, turning paler when old; attached to the stem; with fuzzy edges; often show droplets of clear moisture; gush mild-tasting white milk when bruised; becoming dirty brownish where bruised.

Spore print: White.

Stem: 4" to 6" long, ⅝" to 1 ¼" thick; colored like the cap, but usually paler; gushes mild white milk when cut or broken.

Growth habit: Singly or in groups on the ground in woods.

Edibility: Fine.

Copycats: Brown milky *(Lactarius volemus)* does not have such a wrinkled cap.

Tip: Like orange-brown milky mushrooms, wrinkled milky mushrooms develop a fishy odor after they are picked. To have them at their best, cook them as soon as you can.

---

32 **Blue milk mushroom**
Lactarius indigo (Schweinitz) Fries
(lack-TA-ree-us IN-dih-go)

Of all the strange and weirdly beautiful mushrooms in the world, this one is near the top of the list. Just as I'm moved every year when I see the first fireflies of summer or the blaze of autumn leaves, I'm awestruck every time I find a blue milk mushroom. To come upon such a big mushroom entirely colored bright blue—cap, gills, and stem—is startling, especially for novices who have not seen *Lactarius indigo* before. But the real surprise comes when you bruise or break the mushroom and it oozes blue milk: not so-so blue, or pale blue, or maybe blue, but shocking, electric blue. In my summer mushroom workshop, a woman held a specimen in her blue-stained hand and whispered, "This is my dream mushroom!"

Another surprise for beginners comes when they learn that this is a fine edible species. All mushroom guidebooks praise it. Unless a person cannot see the color blue, this is the easiest mushroom of all to identify. Too bad it's not more common throughout this region.

All parts of the bruised mushroom ooze the blue milk that slowly turns the injured tissue greenish.

In a nutshell:

Large blue to silvery blue mushrooms that ooze blue milk and develop greenish colors from bruising or aging.

Cap: 1 ½" to 6" across. Blue, becoming silvery blue; sometimes with green stains; funnel shaped.

Gills: Blue; attached to stem.

Spore print: Creamy yellowish.

Stem: ¾" to 2 ½" long, ⅜" to 1" thick.

Growth habit: Scattered, often sparsely, on the ground in both oak and pine woods. July to October.

Edibility: Very good.

Copycats: None.

Tip: Some mushroomers color fabric with dyes prepared from various mushrooms. I don't know of an artist who paints with the colored fluids of mushrooms. Your mushroom guidebooks describe species of *Lactarius* that offer a wide range of colored milk, though, and will provide plenty of pigments for your palette.

---

33 **Peppery milk mushroom**
Lactarius piperatus (Fries) S. F. Gray
(lack-TA-ree-us pie-per-RAY-tus)

Known locally as hot mother.

Nature plays practical jokes on a beginning mushroomer. It can happen on a summer day, on an ordinary mushroom-hunting trip. When you get to the woods, you find an extravaganza of plump, snow white, delectable-looking mushrooms that excites your novice heart. Two questions spring to mind: Are these mushrooms edible? And why did I bring such a small basket? You pick a specimen for examination and discover, with relief, that these are definitely not *Amanita* mushrooms. As you carefully break the edge of the cap, pure white milk gushes from the exposed flesh. With moist eyes, you realize that Mother Nature is kindly offering you a taste of her sweet milk. You touch your tongue to a big drop of the white fluid. The taste is mildly sweet and earthy. You feel warm and nurtured, grateful for nature's gifts, and one with the world.

Then a slight burning sensation on the tip of your tongue interrupts your reverie. It grows stronger and begins to spread throughout your mouth. You spit—and spit some more—but spitting does not stop the burning. You grope for your water bottle and remember that you left it in your car, miles away. As the heat intensifies, you run about, looking for a stream to cool your mouth. Blessedly, after a few minutes, the discomfort begins to diminish. In the aftermath, you feel chagrined and deceived, and you begin to rethink your relationship with nature.

I'm telling you this hypothetical story so you won't be another unsuspecting victim of the aptly named peppery milk mushroom or one of its close relatives, like the deceptive milk mushroom *(Lactarius deceptivus)*. Yet sooner or later, almost everyone reading this warning will give in to the temptation, or dare a friend, to taste a drop of the milk just to see if I am telling you the truth. If you do try it, *don't* swallow the milk. It has the engaging capacity to bring up your lunch—abruptly.

With its fiery fluid, you probably think that everyone puts this species near the top of their "no-no" list and ignores it forever. Yet it's never been easy for mushroomers to simply turn their backs on such a big, bulky mushroom that looks so appealing and grows so abundantly. Long ago, they discovered that if you first boil it for several minutes, throw away the water, and then thoroughly cook the mushroom, it is edible—although some authorities disagree. I've tried it, and I rate its culinary quality below the level of bitter cardboard. I don't recommend eating it at all.

In a nutshell: Big, bulky, very common all-white mushrooms with no fuzz; very close gills; gush hot-tasting white milk when broken.

Cap: 2 ½" to 6 ½" across; white; becoming funnel shaped when old; smooth, with no fuzziness anywhere; gushes hot-tasting white milk when broken or bruised.

Gills: White to cream colored; joined to the stem or running down it; very crowded together; gush hot-tasting white milk when bruised.

Spore print: White.

Stem: ¾" to over 3" long, ½" to 1 ¼" thick; white; gushes peppery milk.

Growth habit: Scattered on the ground under hardwood trees. Very common. July to September.

Edibility: Not recommended.

Copycats: *Lactarius deceptivus* has a fuzzy-edged cap. *L. subvellereus*'s gills are closer, and its cap is completely covered with delicate fuzz. Both have peppery white milk and are not recommended for eating.

Tip: Don't get the milk in your eyes. It burns!

---

34 Wine milk mushroom, wine milky

Lactarius subpurpureus Peck
(lack-TA-ree-us sub-pur-pur-REE-us)

Mushrooming is never short on surprises. As you learn about fungi, you will discover that certain mushrooms do some marvelous and unexpected color tricks. The milky mushroom genus, *Lactarius,* hosts quite a few of these magicians. For example, the wine milk mushroom oozes burgundy-colored juice when it is broken open. After a while, the juice and exposed surfaces turn green from exposure to air. These colorful gymnastics help you identify this mushroom, because very few species have this particular feature. To further distinguish the wine milky, the entire mushroom has a wine red color, often with some greenish spots. Sometimes its cap shows a silvery glow or sheen.

Such strange color wizardry may give you the notion that this mushroom is not good to eat. In mushrooming, weirdness is not a guide to edibility. This is a good edible mushroom.

In a nutshell:

Dull wine red mushrooms with greenish stains, oozing wine red juice where broken. Grows on the ground, singly, mainly in hemlock woods.

Cap: 1 ¼" to 3 ¾" across; dull wine red to purplish with greenish stains; often has a silvery sheen; oozes wine red juice that slowly turns greenish.

Gills: Attached to the stem; colored like the cap; ooze wine red juice that slowly becomes greenish.

Spore print: Yellowish.

Stem: 1 ¼" to 3 ¼" across, ¼" to ½" across; slimy in wet weather; colored like the cap, spotted with darker color.

Growth habit: Singly or small groups on the ground, mainly in hemlock but sometimes in pine woods. August to October.

Edibility: Good.

Copycats: Edible *Lactarius paradoxus* oozes burgundy brown milk and has a bluish colored cap.

Tip: In this region, with so many *Lactarius* species, trying to identify all that you find can overwhelm you. Don't give up. The wine milk mushroom and several other milky mushroom species are easy to identify and very good to eat.

---

35 ### Orange-brown lactarius

Lactarius volemus (Fries) Fries
(lack-TA-ree-us vo-LEE-mus)

Known locally as milkie, milker.

In most communities, some knowledgeable people pick wild mushrooms. They may not be interested in studying mushrooms or even own one mushroom book. But they do know one or two, or maybe a few, species very well that they gather every year. Ordinarily, they go for certain widely known mushrooms such as morels, chanterelles, hen of the woods, and so on. You probably know some of these people. They may have inspired your interest in mushrooming.

Some mushroom hunters gather species that most other people have never heard of. In such a place in the central part of this region, morels are scarce, but orange-brown lactarius mushrooms are very common. The residents gave up searching for morels long ago. Instead, they take to the woods in the summer for an informal (and very competitive) milkie mushroom hunt. No one knows who introduced this tradition. Perhaps the founder of the town was a mushroomer who one day proclaimed, "From this time forth, everyone here will go to the woods in the summer and hunt the orange-brown lactarius, which will forever be called the milkie." I won't tell you the name of this community. The residents don't need more competition.

Most people are unfamiliar with the orange-brown lactarius, but mushroomers know that it's one of the best edible wild species and one of the easiest to identify. Fortunately, bugs don't like it. Because its color is more stable than most mushrooms, it tends to look the same whenever you find it. All *Lactarius* species ooze some more or less milky-looking juice when they are broken open, but this species literally gushes volumes of white milk, as its scientific name indicates.

> **In a nutshell:** Orange-brown cap; white gills; whole mushroom gushes white milk when broken; stains brown from bruising and develops a fishy odor after picking.

Cap: 2" to 5" across; dry; smooth; firm and brittle; orange-brown color; oozes lots of mild-tasting white milk where broken; broken tissue becomes brown.

Gills: Attached to the stem or run down it; white, maybe lightly yellow tinged; stain brown from bruising; ooze mild-tasting white milk when bruised or broken.

Spore print: White.

Stem: 1" to 4" long; colored like the cap, but maybe a bit paler; firm, smooth, and usually solid; oozes white milk when broken; bruises and breaks stain brown.

Growth habit: On the ground, often in large groups, in woods and along the road in forests. July to September.

Edibility: Very good if cooked slowly.

Copycats: *Lactarius corrugis* has a wrinkled cap. *L. hygrophoroides*'s gills are noticeably more widely spaced and do not stain brown when bruised. Both are edible. Don't eat any mushroom with an unpleasant tasting milky fluid.

Tip: Don't store the mushrooms too long before you cook them, because they will develop a fishy odor—unless, of course, you like seafood.

---

36 ### American lepiota
Lepiota americana Peck
(leh-pee-OH-tah a-mare-ree-CAN-nah)

Also called *Leucocoprinus americana*.

Certain mushrooms don't try to hide their identity from us. These fungal extroverts make mushroomers very happy by showing us their unique, distinctive features. Some mushroomers wish that all fungi were like this, but others would say that such simplicity would take the fun out of the sport. Fortunately, we have mushrooms to satisfy both kinds of enthusiasts.

The American lepiota is one of the easy ones. Typical of lepiotas, it has white gills that are unattached to the stem and a ring on the stem. But the American lepiota's stem shape is special because it resembles an upright, stretched bowling pin. The mushroom displays unusual colors, too: it shows yellow-orange colors where it's bruised or cut, and it develops wine reddish colors as it ages. In addition, its white cap is adorned with reddish scales.

This mushroom has a long history of edibility, but a novice must be careful. Certainly, the American lepiota is distinctive, but lepiotas have some features of the dangerous *Amanita* genus. Read the description of amanitas in the "Edible and Inedible Mushrooms" section of this book and elsewhere. I have also found a robust form of the American lepiota locally that has a hot flavor and burns the throat. It's almost certainly inedible. Maybe it is a variety of *Lepiota americana,* or perhaps it's a similar-looking species that is not described in any of the guidebooks I have read. Or perhaps the hot taste is related to the nature of the woodchips it grows upon—its favorite food.

> **In a nutshell:**
>
> Large white caps with reddish scales; free white gills; a bowling pin-shaped stem. The whole mushroom bruises yellow-orange when young and becomes reddish with age.

Cap: 1" to 4" across; egg shaped at first, becoming nearly flat when mature, often with a knob in the center; white, with reddish or reddish brown scales; white flesh, bruising yellow-orange at first and becoming red with age.

Gills: Free from the stem; white, becoming reddish or brownish with age.

Spore print: White.

Stem: 3" to 5" long; swollen at the base; with a ring, at least when young; white, bruising yellow-orange when young, becoming reddish with age.

Growth habit: In groups and clumps in wood chip patches and piles, old sawdust, and grassy places. July to October.

Edibility: Very good, but don't confuse it with a toxic amanita. Don't eat it if it's hot flavored.

Copycats: *Amanita rubescens* displays pale flaky warts on the cap, not reddish scales, and lacks the bowling pin–shaped stem. Don't confuse the poisonous green gill mushroom, *Chlorophyllum molybdites,* with the American lepiota. Both possess some similar features, but the green gill gives a green spore print, while the American lepiota gives a white print.

Tip: Check the landscaping wood chip mulch patches around parking lots and public buildings for the American lepiota. It likes to grow in such places.

---

37 **Parasol mushroom**

Macrolepiota procera (Scopoli) Singer
(MACK-row-leh-pee-OH-tah pro-SE-rah)

Also called *Lepiota procera* in some guidebooks.

Because of its sweet maple nut taste and aroma, many mushroomers put the parasol near the top of their "favorite edible mushrooms" list. Almost all mushroom guidebooks include it and describe it as an excellent edible species. Some mushroom collectors prefer to dry parasols before using them. They have learned that dehydration enriches the flavor and strengthens the mushroom's rich aroma.

It's hard to ignore parasol mushrooms. With their large, scaly, almost fuzzy caps, they are real eye-catchers. Sometimes they can grow to huge sizes, with stems over a foot high and caps almost a foot across. Don't expect to bring home many, because they like to grow singly or in small groups. (Besides, they tend to be scarce in most places.)

While this species has a number of distinctive features, beginners must be sure to avoid confusing it with poisonous *Amanita* species. One of the main differences is that parasols have a plain, smooth, unadorned, bulbous swelling at the base of the stem, while *Amanita* species have a sheathlike sack or scaly bulb at the bottom of the stem. Also, the ring on the stem of a parasol is movable and not rigidly attached. *Amanita* stem rings are more firmly attached and do not move easily. Unlike the parasol mushroom's, the *Amanita* species' ring tends to tear apart when you try to move it.

In a nutshell: Big, umbrella-shaped, brownish, scaly caps; a long stem with a ring that moves; a smooth swelling at the base of the stem.

Cap: From about 3" to 12" across; bulb shaped when young, but later expanding to a convex white cap covered with brown spotlike scales and a brown knob in the center of the cap.

Gills: White when young, but becoming slightly darker colored with age; free from the stem.

Spore print: White.

Stem: Long and skinny (5" to 12" long and about ½" thick); whitish; with a movable ring and a smooth bulb at the base.

Edibility: Edible and delicious, but be sure that it is not an amanita.

Growth habit: Singly, or with a few companions, in open places, grassy places, and along the edge of woods. July to September.

Copycats: The edible shaggy parasol mushroom, *Macrolepiota rachodes,* stains red when cut or bruised. Poisonous *Chlorophyllum molybdites* makes a green spore print. Other similar *Lepiota* species have sharp brown scales on the cap that rub off easily. Check *Amanita* species descriptions, too.

Tip: Parasol mushrooms are scarce in many locations, but if you go back to where you have found them previously, you may find them there again. They often reappear in the same place for many years.

---

38 Platterfull mushroom

Megacollybia platyphylla (Persoon : Fries) Kotlaba and Pouzar (meh-ga-co-LIB-ee-ah pla-tee-FYE-lah)

Also called *Tricholomopsis platyphylla, Oudemansiella platyphylla, Collybia platyphylla.*

As you hike through the woods in the warm months of the year, you can't help but notice this sometimes very large mushroom. Bugs love it. They usually make it their home long before you find it. Inside and outside, they can quickly work it over in ways that put off even the most bug-tolerant mushroom collector. You may feel sad that such a big, beautiful edible mushroom is so often wasted as insect food. It's really not much of a loss, though, because the flavor of this species is not very appealing. Besides, it has caused stomach upset for a few people who have eaten it, although I have not met anyone who has that problem.

I have sampled this species a few times when I was lucky enough to beat the bugs. I found it to be bland and mushy. It's probably best to leave it for the insects to enjoy. After all, they need to eat, too.

In a nutshell:

Large mushroom with brown cap; white spore print; gills attached to the stem, which has white cords at the bottom. Grows with rotten wood.

Cap: 3" to 5" or more across; grayish brown; sometimes with the sweet odor of anise.

Gills: White; attached to the stem; broad, far apart, and cracking when old.

Spore print: White.

Stem: 3" to 5" long, ⅜" to ¾" thick; with a tough skin; white rootlike strands attached to the bottom.

Growth habit: In woods, on and around rotting stumps and logs. May to November.

Edibility: Edible.

Copycats: *Pluteus cervinus,* the fawn mushroom, has pink spores and gills unattached to the stem.

Tip: To identify this species, pay particular attention to the gills. Remember that they are widely spaced, unusually broad, and tend to crack and split as they age.

---

39 Common mycena

Mycena galericulata (Fries) S. F. Gray
(my-SENN-na ga-ler-ih-cue-LAY-tah)

Close up, this little mushroom is beautiful, but people often ignore it because it's so unassuming. Although it's not particularly easy to distinguish the common mycena from similar-looking species, you will find it frequently through the summer and into early fall after you become adept at mushroom identification. Few modern guidebooks comment on its edibility, but older authorities report that it is quite safe to eat and delicious, if you can gather enough for a dish (and are confident of your identification). My friends and I have eaten it for many years and enjoy it.

Mycena species are notoriously difficult to identify. Of the hundreds of species in the genus, *M. galericulata* is one of the easier ones. Many are among the tiniest of mushrooms, with caps less than ¼" across. Most people do not notice these, but some mushroomers have a particular interest in little species. These are the fungus hunters you will see searching the woods on their hands and knees. (Now you know that they are not looking for a lost contact lens.)

In a nutshell: Small grayish to brownish mushrooms with long, skinny, pale stems. The edges of the caps turn up when old. Grow on rotting hardwood logs and stumps.

Cap: ¼" to 1 ½" across; drab gray to brown; with fine lines along the surface duplicating the gill pattern beneath; bell shaped when young, but becoming flatter with age, with the edge of the cap uplifted.

Gills: White to pale pink, without spots; delicately depressed at the stem; running down the stem; connected by veins on the underside of the cap.

Spore print: White.

Stem: 2" to 5" long, ¹⁄₁₆" to ¼" thick; long and thin; whitish, but gray at the bottom; hollow.

Growth habit: In clusters on rotting hardwood logs and stumps. June to November.

Edibility: Edible—but be sure of your identification.

Copycats: *Mycena maculata* develops pink spots on the gills when old. *M. alcalina* smells like chlorine bleach. *M. inclinata* has a white speckled stem that is rusty brown at the bottom.

Tip: Details of the gills are important in identifying this mushroom. They can become pinkish when old, but they don't develop pink spots. Look for the tiny notch, or depression, where the gills join the stem and for their tendency to run down the stem. Also notice the crossing veins that connect the gills on the underside of the cap. A magnifying glass will help.

40 ## Jack o' lantern

Omphalotus olearius (De Candolle : Fries) Singer
(om-fa-LOW-tus owe-lee-A-ree-us)

Older books will list it as *Omphalotus illudens* and *Clitocybe illudens.*

The name jack o' lantern fits this fascinating mushroom nicely, because it grows in big pumpkin-colored orange clusters that glow in the dark with an eerie green light. Daytime or nighttime, everyone notices them. The often huge mushrooms look delectable, but don't take them home for dinner because they cause nausea and vomiting. People who have eaten them often report a strange slight burning sensation in their throats when swallowing. That alone should have been a warning that something was not right. Reckless optimism and mushrooming don't mix.

Poisonings from mushrooms are infrequent, here or anywhere. In this region, the jack o' lantern is the most common culprit. Usually it happens when an impetuous beginning mushroomer, with unbridled enthusiasm, mistakes it for the golden chanterelle *(Cantharellus cibarius)*. Yet the two species display distinct differences. For one thing, the golden chanterelle typically is entirely egg yolk yellow to orange-yellow in color, but the jack o' lantern mushroom is bright orange. Also, chanterelles grow on the ground, while the wood-eating jack o' lantern prefers to grow on or at the base of tree stumps. Chanterelles grow singly or in groups, but the jack o' lantern tends to grow in dense clusters. Finally, the chanterelle has a clearly forked and branched gill-like underside, while the gills of jack o' lanterns do not fork.

I believe that mushroom guidebooks do not always make clear the variable appearance of the chanterelle, which is a major reason for beginners' confusing the two species. Books tend to emphasize the chanterelle's yellow color, but sometimes they don't emphasize that you can also find this species colored orange-yellow in certain parts of the United States (such as this region). Guidebooks also generally describe the chanterelle's underside as covered with thick, blunt-edged wrinkles, but the most

> **In a nutshell:**
>
> Large, entirely orange mushrooms with luminescent gills running down the stem. Grow in clusters on buried wood, usually at the base of stumps.

common variety here has knife-edge–shaped gills, like the jack o' lantern's.

The same chemical reactions that give a firefly its bioluminescence (that is, its biological light) cause the jack o' lantern's magical glow. Both produce a protein called luciferin and an enzyme called luciferase. When these two biochemical agents react, they release energy as visible light. Appropriately and poetically, these chemicals are named for Lucifer, the mythical light bearer. Only the underside of the mushroom glows—sometimes brightly enough to read a newspaper by after your eyes have adapted to the dark.

Cap: 3" to 6" across; orange to yellow-orange colored; often with an irregularly shaped edge.

Gills: Same color as the cap; running down the stem; knife-edge shaped, not branched or forked.

Spore print: White or yellow-cream tinted.

Stem: 3" to 9" long, ⅜" to ⅝" thick; same color as the cap.

Edibility: Poisonous.

Growth habit: In clusters on or around hardwood stumps or buried wood. June to September.

Copycats: It resembles the chanterelle (see above). It also resembles the false chanterelle *(Hygrophoropsis aurantiaca),* which grows on the ground, not wood, and has forked gills.

Tip: For a novel kind of bedroom excitement, bring jack o' lantern mushrooms home and place them on your nightstand. If you can stay awake long enough to let your eyes adapt to the dark, you can revel in the all-night light show. The mushrooms deteriorate quickly at room temperatures, however, and lose their glow. If you store the mushrooms in a paper bag in your refrigerator through the day and bring them out at night, you can keep the mushrooms fresh longer and enjoy more midnight fireworks.

---

41 **Rooted xerula, rooted oudemansiella, rooted collybia**
Xerula radicata (Rehlan : Fries) Dörfelt var. *radicata*
(zer-OO-la ra-dih-CAY-tah)

You will find this species named *Oudemansiella radicata* and *Collybia radicata* in some guidebooks.

It's hard to think of a better word than "rooted" to name this mushroom. Like a carrot or dandelion plant, it sends down a long taprootlike stem extension into the ground. You can't unearth the fragile root without the right tool, such a hand shovel. If you can't see the root, you will miss a significant feature of this very common edible mushroom. (The photo included here does not show it well, because the specimen was dug with a pocketknife.)

Aside from the deep taproot, other earmarks help you learn to recognize the rooted xerula. Its unusually brittle, long, thin stem easily snaps like a matchstick. As the cap turns upward with age, it displays the widely spaced broad white gills. Look for it on and around hardwood stumps, especially beech. It often covers a large area, growing from buried roots.

When you first eat the rooted xerula, you may disagree with the many guidebooks that comment on its poor quality. You may wonder whether the authors really did sample the mushroom or merely copied others' remarks. Cook it briskly in a hot pan for the best flavor. Then make your own decision.

In a nutshell: Brownish colored, smooth, slightly slimy caps that turn upward when old; white, widely spaced gills; a long, brittle stem with a deep root.

Cap: 1" to 4" across; brown to yellowish or grayish brown; smooth but sometimes wrinkled at the edge; slightly sticky when moist; turns upward when old.

Gills: White and shiny; widely spaced; broad; of various lengths; depressed at the stem.

Spore print: White.

Stem: 2" to 8" long, ⅛" to ⅜" thick; brittle; usually smooth; narrower at the top; white at the top, and brown lower; with a deep, pointed, taprootlike stem extension.

Growth habit: Single or scattered, from underground dead roots and around hardwood trees and stumps, especially beech. July to October.

Edibility: Good.

Copycats: *Xerula furfuracea* has a scaly stem. *X. megalospora* smells like carrots or geranium. Both are edible. When the stem of *X. rubrobrunnescens* is bruised, it stains rusty.

Tip: People who enjoy dandelion leaves for salad know that they can harvest successive crops if they leave the taproot in the ground. Not so for the rooted xerula. After you pick the mushroom, another mushroom will not grow from the same root. You have not killed the fungus, however. More mushrooms will come from the fungus's underground parts soon afterwards or next summer.

---

42 **Fuzzy foot**

Paxillus atrotomentosus (Batsch : Fries) Fries
(pack-SILL-lus a-troe-toe-men-TOE-sus)

Don't trust the older guidebooks when they tell you that the fuzzy foot is safe to eat. Many mushroom authorities have become very suspicious about it. A related species, *Paxillus involutus,* was thought to be safe, too, but it has caused a number of deaths. So mycologists warn not to eat the fuzzy foot mushroom until further studies determine its safety.

Some readers will scoff at this recommendation. Here and in Europe, both species have been collected for food for generations. I know mushroomers who have eaten them all their lives with no ill effects. Yet it's a fact that some people develop a particular sensitivity after eating *P. involutus* that can cause fatal poisoning if they eat it again after a certain period of time. Mycologists worry that the fuzzy foot may have the same properties. I used to eat the fuzzy foot frequently, but I stopped when I began to see warnings that it, too, may not be safe.

Its fat, dark brown, fuzzy stem, tan gills that run down the stem, and habit of growing on wood help make this common mushroom species easy to identify. Sometimes, the fuzz of the stem is so thick that it looks almost hairy. Look for it in parks and picnic areas, where it likes to grow best.

In a nutshell:

Big, bulky, tough, brown-capped, wood-growing mushroom with a thick, brown, very fuzzy stem. Its yellowish gills run down the stem and peel easily from the cap.

Cap: 1 ½" to 8" across; brown, slightly fuzzy; feels dry when touched.

Gills: Tan or yellowish; running down the stem; easily peeled as a layer from the cap.

Spore print: Yellowish.

Stem: ¾" up to 4" long, ½" to 1 ¼" thick; tough; brown, covered with dark brown, dense fuzz.

Growth habit: Grows on conifer stumps and buried wood. July to October.

Edibility: Avoid it. It may be poisonous.

Copycats: None. It is quite distinct.

Tip: Do not eat this mushroom until it has been studied further.

---

43 **Firm russula**

Russula compacta Frost
(RUSS-su-lah com-PACK-tah)

After looking over your guidebooks' descriptions of the general features of *Russula* species, you may think that all of them have delicate, splintery gills and soft, brittle stems. Then you find a mushroom like the firm russula. Suddenly you must change your conception of *Russula,* because this species definitely has a tougher, coarser texture than you expected to find. You also soon learn that it and a number of other similarly firm-fleshed russulas tend to be inedible or poor choices for the dinner table.

The difficulty of identifying russulas is well known, but the firm russula waves a flag by developing a distinctive rusty brown color on the gills from bruising. It also has a particularly strong, unpleasant, almost fishy odor, at least in old age. Their abundance of growth can be astonishing. Sometimes you'll see the floor of a conifer forest carpeted with large, firm, rusty brown, dry-surfaced caps.

In a nutshell: Firm, large, white (becoming reddish brown) caps; whitish gills and stem; bruises rusty brown. Grows on the ground.

Cap: 1 ½" to 7" across; hard texture; white, but becoming tan to reddish brown from the center; bruises rusty brown.

Gills: Whitish, bruising rusty brown.

Spore print: White.

Stem: 1 ¼" to 3 ½" long, ½" to 1 ⅜" thick; white and hard; bruises rusty brown.

Growth habit: Singly or scattered on the ground in conifer woods. July to September.

Edibility: Poor. It is best avoided.

Copycats: A number of *Russula* species of this region that stain when bruised resemble the firm russula in form and structure. These bruise red, black, or gray, however— not rusty brown.

Tip: Older guidebooks may tell you that the firm russula is good to eat. The best current advice is to avoid it.

---

44 Crusty russula

Russula crustosa Peck*
(RUSS-su-lah cruss-STOE-sah)

This *Russula* species is like a chameleon. The cap can have a different color every time you find it. One time, it will have rusty yellow colors. Next time, it may be purple, or gray. Or brown. Or yellow-green. Or a combination of any or all of these colors, and perhaps more. This kind of quick-change artistry often means identification problems for beginners. Yet with all this color trickery, the crusty russula is easy to know: its colorful crusty-looking cap surface gives it away.

Without color vision, distinguishing this mushroom from its close relative, the green russula *(Russula virescens)*, would be difficult. Both species' caps are decorated—or, in some observers' opinion, marred— with crusty- or moldy-looking patches. The crusty russula, however, does not develop the dark green colors of the green russula. Look, too, for the fine radial lines, duplicating the underside gill pattern, along the edge of the crusty's cap. The green russula tends to not show these, except sometimes weakly in old age. Another difference is the crusty's pale yellow-orange spore print color. Both of these russulas are fine to eat.

In a nutshell: Brittle mushroom with moldy-looking cap; green and other colors.

Cap: 2" to 6" across; greenish through yellow, tan, brown and purple colors; with a patchy or crusty surface;

with fine radial lines along the edge of the cap (called a "striate margin").

Gills: White when young, yellowish with age; some forked; attached to the stem.

Spore print: Pale yellow-orange.

Stem: 1" to 3 ⅛" long, ⅝" to over 1 ½" thick; white; becoming hollow in old age.

Growth habit: Singly or in small groups on the ground in woods. July to August.

Edibility: Very good.

Copycats: The green russula *(R. virescens)* does not develop yellow or orange cap colors and has a pale yellow spore print.

Tip: When a green russula *(R. virescens)* gets old, its dark green cap color can fade, sometimes making it hard to distinguish from an aged crusty russula. A spore print will help distinguish the two: white to pale yellow for the green, and pale yellow-orange for the crusty.

* Name derived from G. H. Lincoff, *National Audubon Society Field Guide to North American Mushrooms* (New York: Knopf, 1997).

---

45 Fragrant russula

Russula laurocerasi Melzer
(RUSS-su-lah lar-roe-se-RASS-see)

Some older guidebooks, perhaps incorrectly, call this fungus *Russula foetens.*

When you first pick a fragrant russula and smell its mouthwatering maraschino cherry fragrance, you will want to run home, cut it up, and sprinkle it on ice cream. Not so fast. I've found no one who recommends that you eat this mushroom—not even the older authorities who were often inclined to give certain doubtfully edible mushrooms a break. Practically everyone who has tried this russula reports that it tastes just *awful.* It may even be poisonous. Sometimes, nature can be cruel.

In a nutshell:

Maraschino cherry–scented, slimy, yellow-colored mushroom, often with little droplets of moisture on yellowish gills.

A second sniff will often reveal a subtle, nauseating background odor. Here is another initially appealing mushroom that doesn't even make it to the lowest level of your edible list. A number of related species have a more or less similar odor and appearance, and these are definite no-nos, too.

Cap: 1" to 5" across; yellow to dull yellow-brown; slimy; brittle; with rough lines along the edge of the cap, duplicating the gill pattern beneath.

Gills: Yellowish white, developing brownish spots with time; often covered with small clear droplets of moisture; attached to the stem.

Spore print: Pale orange-yellow.

Stem: 1" to 4 ⅛" long, ⅜" to 1" thick; yellowish white, becoming stained with yellowish brown to brown splotches.

Growth habit: Singly or in small groups on the ground under hardwood and conifer trees. July to September.

Edibility: Inedible.

Copycats: *Russula foetens* may not grow in the United States, but is often mistaken for this species. *R. fragrantissima* is larger and darker, smells awful, and when raw, tastes strongly hot. *R. subfoetens* is smaller and has a bright rusty orange to rusty brown cap. All are inedible.

Tip: If it really bothers you that you can't eat this mushroom, you can always buy white button mushrooms and maraschino cherries from the supermarket and cook them together. Then you can pretend that you are eating fragrant russulas.

---

46 **Variable russula**
Russula variata Banning*
(RUSS-su-la va-ree-AY-tah)

Sometimes the *Russula* genus, the home of so many perplexing species, smiles kindly upon hard-working mushroomers and offers an easily identifiable species. You may think that a mushroom named *variata*, indicating diversity of appearance, would cause identification problems. Yet even with its variations, this mushroom has certain distinct features. The cap displays peculiar dull tones of green and/or pink and often purple. The conspicuously forked gills, which may branch two or three times along their length, offer one of the most distinguishing earmarks. Although hot-tasting when raw, the variable russula generally loses its peppery qualities and becomes edible after cooking. Many mushroomers don't enjoy the flavor, though, and it can occasionally taste unpleasantly bitter. Sometimes, an uncomfortable peppery taste stays even after long cooking. So along with the changeable cap colors, its edibility seems to vary, too.

 In a nutshell: Sizeable mushroom with dull green, pink, and purplish cap tones and conspicuously forked gills.

Cap: 2" to 6" across; very variable in color, but usually showing mixed drab tones of green, dull purple, pink, and yellow; brittle.

Gills: White; forked; attached to the stem.

Spore print: White.

Stem: 1" to 4" long, ⅜" to 1 ¼" thick; white; hollow in old age.

Growth habit: Singly or in small groups on the ground in woods. July to October.

Edibility: Edible.

Copycats: Its range of dull cap colors and its forked gills set it apart.

Tip: Because of the variability of the flavor, you may want to check out the quality of your basket of variable russulas before you commit them to an elaborate dish, especially if you plan to share it with friends or family.

* Name derived from G. H. Lincoff, *National Audubon Society Field Guide to North American Mushrooms* (New York: Knopf, 1997).

---

47 **Green russula**
Russula virescens Fries*
(RUSS-su-lah vih-RESS-sens)

Known locally as moldy russula.

After a good look, you're not likely to forget this highly praised edible mushroom because of the moldy-looking green patches that cover the cap surface. Your first impression may be that it certainly looks weird, and maybe even beautiful in a way, but who would want to put something like that in his or her mouth? After you become fully confident of your identification and dare to put it in the frying pan for a taste test, you will change your mind. Like most mushroomers, you will be impressed with the fine flavor—and it will become one of your favorite edible mushrooms.

To most mushroomers, the green russula is the best edible species of the genus and one of the easiest to learn. No one can ignore russulas, because they are among the most brightly colored mushrooms you'll see. Unfortunately, subtle and variable differences among many of the species cause identification problems. To further complicate matters, authorities have not yet named many russulas that you will find in your outings.

It's a mycological hassle to identify many species of the genus, but it's easy to know if you have found a russula. Typically, russulas make white to yellow spore prints; they have dry, brittle flesh; their gills shatter easily; their brittle stems can snap like a piece of chalk; and they do not exude milk or fluids from the broken flesh. If you come upon a mushroom with these features, you can be pretty sure that you have found a russula.

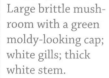

In a nutshell:

Large brittle mushroom with a green moldy-looking cap; white gills; thick white stem.

Cap: 2" to 6" across; brittle; green. The surface cracks into moldy-looking patches.

Gills: White.

Spore print: White to yellowish.

Stem: 1 ¼" to 3 ½" long, ⅜" to ¾" thick; white, smooth, and brittle.

Growth habit: Scattered on the ground in hardwood forests, especially oak and beech. July to August.

Edibility: Very good. Perhaps the best-tasting *Russula* species.

Copycats: The crusty russula (*Russula crustosa*) shows a wider range of cap colors, frequently with yellow or orange tones. It also has a pale yellow-orange spore print.

Tip: You can spend many frustrating hours working with the best available books to identify the *Russula* species you bring home. Don't despair if you can't come up with the names for most of them. Pat yourself on the back for those that you can confidently identify. There are not many russula experts.

* Name derived from G. H. Lincoff, *National Audubon Society Field Guide to North American Mushrooms* (New York: Knopf, 1997).

Neither gilled nor pored

48 **Vase-shaped puffball**
Calvatia cyathiformis (Bosc) Morgan
(cal-VAY-sha sye-a-thih-FOR-miss)

You may wake up one late summer morning and see what looks like large tan cobblestones scattered about your lawn. Before you scold the kids for messing up the landscape, take a closer look and give one of the stones a poke. If it's soft and fleshy, you most likely host a crop of puffball mushrooms—probably vase-shaped puffballs. After a moment of silent reflection, it's almost traditional for non-mushroomers to wind up and give the biggest puffball a good kick, just to watch the explosion of white stuff. Or, if they find them late and punt the puffballs after they ripen, they are rewarded with an exhilarating, huge cloud of dark spores. Either way, it's a fun sport, handed down from generations of puffball kickers, taught to children from their earliest years.

Puffballs are typically squat, roundish, pudgy, thin-skinned mushrooms that form their spores inside. Everyone seems to love them, kickers and non-kickers alike. When young, the edible species (such as the vase-shaped puffball) are typically cream cheese white inside. Most mushroomers like their flavor, but the marshmallow-like texture puts off some people. As they mature and the spores ripen, the interior discolors. Eventually, the mushroom becomes a soft dust bag full of dark spores, ready for the slightest physical disturbance to release a puff of spore smoke.

It's easy to tell if you have the vase-shaped puffball growing in your lawn. It's the only big, purple-spored, lawn-growing puffball that leaves a wide-mouthed vase–shaped base after the top of the mushroom has disintegrated. These vases often overwinter to decorate your lawn after the snow melts in the spring. To be certain of your identification, check all of the mushroom's features.

 In a nutshell: Large, roundish forms; white to tan outside, white inside; developing purple spores.

Detail: 2 ½" to 8" across; round, upside-down-pear shaped; white to tan surface that develops brown patchy spots; white inside when young, becoming filled with purple spore dust when old; leaves a purple vase-shaped base over the winter.

Spore color: Purple.

Growth habit: On the ground in grassy places. August to October.

Edibility: Good when young and white inside.

Copycats: No other lawn-growing large puffball has purple spores and leaves a purple vase-shaped cup after it disintegrates.

Tip: It's a sad situation if you are a mushroomer and puffballs do not grow in your lawn every year. You can try to establish them there the way a number of mushroomers have successfully done. Bring home a large, ripe puffball, loaded with spores, and invite the family to a backyard soccer game. By halftime, you will have spread millions of spores in your lawn and in lawns for blocks around. Expect good puffball picking for years to come—and a lot of kicking practice around the neighborhood.

---

49 **Chanterelle, golden chanterelle**
Cantharellus cibarius Fries
(can-tha-RELL-lus sih-BAR-ree-us)

If you appreciate fine dining, then you can't beat having lots of companions who are experts in the kitchen. As a mushroomer, you have a way to make many of these acquaintances. Simply let it get around the community that you are a chanterelle hunter.

Around the world, chefs love chanterelles. They work magic with them. When the mushroom is available, the world's finest restaurants feature it. Next time you collect a basket of chanterelles, take it to the best restaurant in your community, and invite a good friend to come along. Give the basket to the head chef and ask him or her to prepare a dinner for the two of you. Tell the chef to keep any chanterelles that are left over. You will make three people—the chef, your friend, and yourself—very happy.

Chanterelles are scarce because they cannot be cultivated. Professional and amateur mushroomers collect them in their season from wild places. Like many mushrooms, they require the presence of certain other living things to survive. If you figure out how to grow them commercially, you will become very rich.

For a mushroomer, this species has much to offer. Many of them can grow in one place. Typically, they have a beautiful egg yolk yellow color, and they retain their delightful rose-apricot fragrance after cooking. Fortunately, they tend to come up in the same places, year after year.

In a nutshell:

Bright egg yolk yellow mushroom with pale yellowish spores and a pleasant rose-apricot fragrance. Grows on the ground, never on wood.

Cap: 1" to 3" across; egg yolk yellow color with a rose-apricot fragrance; firm and fleshy; becomes funnel shaped.

Gills: Egg yolk yellow; run down the stem; sometimes thick, with blunt edges.

Spore print: Pale yellow.

Stem: 1" to 2" long, ¼" to ½" thick; firm and solid; egg yolk yellow.

Growth habit: On the ground, sometimes in large groups, in woods and open places. June to September.

Edibility: Excellent.

Copycats: The toxic jack o' lantern mushroom (*Omphalotus olearius*) is bright orange and grows in clusters on or at the base of stumps. Edible cinnabar chanterelles (*Cantharellus cinnabarinus*) are smaller and bright pink. *Hygrophoropsis aurantiaca,* the false chanterelle, is orange in color and does not have the rose-apricot odor of the golden chanterelle. In this area, however, you may find an orange-yellow variety of the golden chanterelle, so check your descriptive details carefully.

Tip: Don't dry chanterelles to preserve them. They can get tough and woody.

---

50 ### Cinnabar chanterelle, pink chanterelle

Cantharellus cinnabarinus Schweinitz
(can-tha-RELL-lus sin-na-ba-RYE-nus)

Cinnabar is a bright pink-red, almost flamingo-colored ore of mercury. I offer this information not only as a piece of trivia with which you can impress your friends, but also as a clue to how the cinnabar chanterelle got its name. If you know your minerals, you won't have much trouble learning to identify this mushroom when you see it, because it is entirely colored like cinnabar—cap, gills, and stem. Yet color isn't the only feature that makes identification easy. This mushroom also has the typical blunt-edged gills of the chanterelle, gills that fork and branch and run down the stem.

Cinnabar chanterelles are beautiful in form and hue, and they taste as good as they look. Cooks love the fine flavor and the way they add color to a dish. They taste similar to the famous golden chanterelle, but their texture is more tender. Gathering them is more tedious, unfortunately, because of their smaller size. Nor are they as common as their golden brother, especially in the northern parts of this region. Still, they can grow in large patches. I once saw a carpet of cinnabar chanterelles about thirty feet wide and seventy-five feet long. Their dense growth made it hard to take a step without walking on the mushrooms. Mushroomers ordinarily see scenes like this only in their best dreams.

In a nutshell: Small, bright reddish pink, funnel-shaped mushrooms with blunt, forked gills that run down the stem.

Cap: ⅜" to 1 ½" across; becoming funnel shaped, with a wavy edge; flamingo pink or cinnabar colored.

Gills: Run down the stem; thick and blunt; branching and forking; colored like the cap.

Spore print: Pinkish cream.

Stem: ½" to 1 ½" long, ⅛" to ¼" thick; colored like the cap, but sometimes duller.

Growth habit: In patches, mainly along mossy trails in oak woods. June into October.

Edibility: Very good.

Copycats: *Hygrophorus* species have waxy-looking sharp-edged gills.

Tip: To see the cinnabar chanterelle's unusual pinkish creamy spore color most clearly, make the spore print on the whitest paper you can find and view it in daylight.

---

51 **Small chanterelle**
Cantharellus minor Peck
(can-tha-RELL-lus MY-nor)

Many mushroomers consider this little mushroom as delicious as the famous golden chanterelle. Although tiny—usually not more than one and a half inches across—sometimes you can find lots of small chanterelles. Any amount can be a special addition to a dish because of the fine flavor and bright yellow color.

You can scramble your brains, though, when you read the different descriptions of this mushroom in your various guidebooks—so get the aspirin ready. The only thing guidebook authors seem to agree on is that *Cantharellus minor* is a small yellow chanterelle. Details of the gills seem to be particularly mysterious. One guidebook will present the gills as sharp edged, like knife blades. Another describes them as blunt and dull edged. Some say that the gills are rarely forked and branched, while others tell you that they are strongly forked. Still others say that cross veins connect the gills, and—you guessed it—yet another reports that the mushroom gills do not have cross veins. It's truly amazing how such a humble little mushroom causes so much consternation among mushroom authorities.

In a nutshell:

Small, bright yellow, funnel-shaped mushrooms; gills that run down the stem; white spores.

I won't get into the disagreements over its growing season, size, and color range. Either a wide range of variations of the species occupies the woods, or more likely, there are many similar-looking small yellow *Cantharellus* species. People eat these all the time without any trouble, thinking that they are *Cantharellus minor,* so even the misidentified ones seem to be edible.

Cap: ½" to 1 ½" across; yellow; funnel shaped; smooth; edge often wavy.

Gills: Yellow; extend down the stem.

Spore print: White.

Stem: 1" to ½" long, ¹⁄₁₆" thick or even thinner; yellow; smooth; becomes hollow with age.

Edibility: Edible and good.

Growth habit: On the ground, in groups and sometimes small clusters, in open woods. June to July.

Copycats: There are many more or less similar small yellow chanterelles.

Tip: It seems that many similar-looking small yellow chanterelles are edible. It's dangerous to be loose and flexible with the descriptive details of mushrooms, however.

---

52 Golden fairy spindle

Clavulinopsis fusiformis (Fries) Corner
(clav-you-lie-NOP-sis few-sih-FOR-miss)

Listed as *Clavaria fusiformis* in older guidebooks.

In their flights of fancy, mushroomers have described this bizarre and lovely mushroom as tongues of flame, slender golden fingers, yellow-colored coral, and more. When you examine this miniature species closely, you may feel that these poetic images are well chosen. Some of the smallest fungi are truly beautiful, but you won't be able to appreciate them unless you take the time to look them over carefully, close up. You may have to get down on your hands and knees to do it, though.

Anyone with their eyes to the ground in the woods in summer has seen this brightly colored fungus.

Mushroomers who enjoy a plate of fungi will think yes, it certainly is a beautiful mushroom and almost too small to collect for a meal, but I can't help wondering . . . can I eat it? The answer, according to many authorities, is "yes," but it may taste bitter.

Golden fairy spindle is an old name for this mushroom. Long ago, everyone knew what "spindle" meant, but we don't hear the word used much anymore. It's a slender wooden rod that was used to twist fibers into thread when people spun wool by hand.

> **In a nutshell:**
>
> Small, bright yellow, dense clusters of fleshy thin fingers. Often grows from one base.

Detail: 2" to 4" high, only ⅛" to ½" thick; bright lemon yellow; skinny worm- or finger-shaped forms, sometimes flattened, often branched, growing in dense tufts.

Spore print: White to yellowish.

Growth habit: In damp places and humus, usually in dense tufts. July to October.

Edibility: Edible.

Copycats: A number of closely related species have a similar form, but they tend not to show the entirely bright yellow color of the golden fairy spindle. *Clavulinopsis helveola* is more delicate.

Tip: Add golden fairy spindles to jars of pickled vegetables for a spark of color.

---

53 **Horn of plenty, black trumpets, woods truffle**
Craterellus fallax Smith
(cray-ter-RELL-lus FAL-lax)

Known locally as trumpets.

It's fun to take beginning mushroomers hunting for black trumpets. You can stand in a huge patch of beautiful fresh trumpets and your novice friends may not see them, even if you tell them that the mushrooms are practically underfoot. They look so much like last year's dark, wilted tree leaves that even some experienced mushroomers must focus their attention to spot them. I don't like to admit it, but at times, after many years of mushrooming, I have walked right by without noticing them when I was thinking about other things. When you hunt for black trumpets, you have to be on your toes.

Not so for some of my chef friends, who consider this species to be the very best of all the edible mushrooms. They have honed their trumpet-spotting abilities and can see them even from a distance. During the times of warm summer rains, they head for the woods with the hope of collecting the year's supply. One of my mushroomer friends even hunts them from horseback. Now that takes some skill!

Often, I hear strange comments from beginners when they see their first black trumpets: "Do you really *eat* these things?" It's true—they really don't look edible. But it doesn't take long to learn to love them, as trumpet addicts can attest.

 In a nutshell: Black or dark brown, trumpet-shaped, fleshy mushroom with a wrinkled outside surface.

Detail: Trumpet shaped; 1 ¼" to 6" high, ⅜" to 3 ½" wide across the mouth; fleshy, with an outside surface that ranges from nearly smooth to wrinkled; black, gray, or dark brown.

Spore print: Rust colored.

Growth habit: On the ground, often in moss, in dense groups under hardwood trees. August to September.

Edibility: Excellent, fresh or dried.

Copycats: *Craterellus cornucopioides* makes a white spore print. *Cantharellus cinereus* has blunt, forked gills. Both are called black trumpets, too. Both are edible and taste similar to *Craterellus fallax*.

Tip: It's hard to confuse black trumpets with any other mushrooms. You can easily learn to identify them by yourself, if you have some descriptive guidebooks with good illustrations.

---

54 ## Bird's nest fungus

Crucibulum laeve (Hudson) Kamby
(crew-SIH-byu-lum LAY-ve)

Has also been called *Crucibulum levis* and *Crucibulum vulgare*.

This is a mushroom for children and for every grown-up who still has the eyes of a child. Most of us, absorbed in the business of life, rarely bother to glance twice at this tiny, inconspicuous fungus scattered about the ground on decaying twigs and vegetable debris. But an astonishing sight rewards those who take the time to get down to the ground for a close look. Each little mushroom, about the size of the tip of a child's little finger, looks remarkably like a tiny bird's nest with several little white eggs. (I've wondered what kind of miniature bird a child might imagine to lay such eggs.)

Scientifically, the eggs are called peridioles (pe-RID-dee-oles), and each contains a mass of spores. The egg dispersal mechanics of the bird's nest fungus are as amazing as its appearance. The nest, called a peridium (pe-RID-dee-um)—and less technically, a "splash cup"—is ideally contoured for efficient egg dispersal by raindrops. Each drop of rain that hits a cup can throw the eggs up to several feet away. Each egg has a sticky thread that attaches it to something. Under good conditions, the spores germinate as the egg case decomposes. If nutrients are available, new colonies of bird's nests develop.

In a nutshell:

Small, white, bird's nest–shaped cups with white interiors and brownish shaggy outsides; contain several small, flattened, white "eggs" with attached sticky cords.

Detail: Nestlike cups ¼" to ⅜" high, ¼" to ⅜" across the top; smooth and shiny white inside, yellowish to brown and shaggy outside when young, but becoming smoother with age. Each cup contains several 1 mm to 2 mm white, flattened, egglike bodies. Grows on rotting wood and decomposing vegetable material.

Edibility: Inedible.

Growth habit: Scattered on vegetable debris. July to October.

Copycats: *Crucibulum parvulum* is smaller and paler colored on the outside of the nest. *Cyathus striatus* shows vertical lines inside the nest and has dark-colored eggs.

Tip: You may be able to grow a bird's nest garden in a jar. Next time you find the fungus, bring some home. Soak some clean crushed peanut shells for a couple of hours in distilled water or rainwater. Then, drain and fill a pint jar about one-quarter of the way up with the moist shells. With a narrow-tipped knife or other pointed tool, carefully remove some eggs and, without handling them with your fingers, place them on the shells. Put a lid on the jar to retain the humidity, but leave it loose enough for ventilation. Add a bit of water now and then if the shells seem to be drying. Eventually, some bird's nests may appear.

---

55   Orange jelly

Dacrymyces palmatus (Schweinitz) Bresadola
(da-cri-MY-sees pal-MAY-tus)

Like weird little globs of bright orange-yellow jelly, the orange jelly mushroom appears to ooze from cracks and hollows in old conifer wood logs and stumps. You'll see it frequently in this region. It's one of our most common species, and it grows from spring all the way into early winter. Few mushrooms have such a long season. Many mushroomers mistake it for the similar-looking witch's butter mushroom, *Tremella mesenterica.* Witch's butter, however, grows on old hardwood, not conifer wood; is more yellow in color; and is not as common as orange jelly in this region. This and other look-alike species can make identification as difficult as nailing jelly to a tree for a beginner. Adventurous mushroomers who experiment with strange and otherworldly-looking mushrooms don't seem to have problems when they confuse these very similar-looking species. All are edible, apparently. Orange jelly, however, can challenge the best cook. Like many other jelly mushrooms, they are flavorless, gummy, and watery. Sautéing reduces them to pasty goo.

In a nutshell: Globby, orange, jellylike clusters oozing from conifer logs and stumps.

Detail: Looks like clusters of chewed-up orange gumdrops; white where they join the wood.

Spore print: Yellowish.

Edibility: Edible, raw or cooked.

Growth habit: From cracks and depressions in old conifer logs and stumps. May to November.

Copycats: Witch's butter, *Tremella mesenterica,* is yellow, not orange, and grows on hardwood. *T. foliacea* is larger and brown. Both species are edible. *Peniophora rufa* is red and waxy looking.

Tip: Orange jelly is edible uncooked, and some mushroomers prefer to eat it raw. It's fun to shock a novice mushroomer by cutting a handful of the alien-looking stuff from a stump and popping it into your mouth on the spot.

---

56 Scaly chanterelle, woolly chanterelle

Gomphus floccosus (Schweinitz) Singer
(GOM-fuss flo-COE-sus)

Referred to as *Cantharellus floccosus* in older books.

I can feel the ground shaking with rumblings of disapproval when I say that you shouldn't eat the scaly chanterelle. Many mushroomers enjoy this mushroom every summer without any trouble—but not all mushroomers. Moreover, a number of older guidebooks say that all chanterelles (mainly species of *Cantharellus, Craterellus,* and *Gomphus*), bar none, are good to eat. Many modern writers agree, but most authorities exclude the scaly chanterelle. They advise avoiding it unless you want to risk severe stomach upset. If you want to test your own sensitivity, do it cautiously (see the "Edible and Non-Edible Mushrooms" section of this book). Personally, I have experienced no ill effects from eating this species.

The distinctive funnel shape, bright orange scaly cap, and pale wrinkled outside make it easy to recognize. To some people, it looks like Sherlock Holmes's calabash pipe. A mushroomer's mouth can water on sight from its inviting chanterelle-like form and longtime reputation for fine flavor. Unfortunately, this large, abundant, eye-catching chanterelle is on most up-to-date no-no lists.

Older guidebooks list the scaly chanterelle as a *Cantharellus* species. Partly because of its vase shape, more wrinkled exterior, and rusty-colored spores, it's now classified as a species of *Gomphus*.

> **In a nutshell:**
>
> Trumpet or vase shaped; orange or reddish yellow and soft-scaly inside; outside, pale rusty yellow; deeply wrinkled and branched.

Cap: 2" to 6" across; deep funnel- or trumpet-shaped form; reddish orange to yellow-orange with large, soft scales.

Gills: Pale rusty yellow; thick, narrow, close, and heavily forking, like thick, deep wrinkles; run strongly down the stem.

Spore print: Dull rusty color.

Stem: 1 ¼" to 4" long, ⅜" to 1 ¼" thick; pale white to yellow-orange; looks like an extension of the cap.

Growth habit: Scattered or in clusters on the ground under conifer trees. July to September.

Edibility: Not recommended.

Copycats: Hard to confuse with anything else. Edible *Craterellus cantharellus* does not have gills, only a wrinkled underside. *Gomphus clavatus* (see below) often shows violet colors when young.

Tip: Don't confuse the scaly chanterelle with the pig's ear (*Gomphus clavatus*) mushroom. The cap of the pig's ear is tan and sometimes tinted violet, and its wrinkled outside usually shows some shade of violet. It's fine flavored and edible for some mushroomers, but causes severe gastric upset for others. Too bad.

---

57 **Yellow jelly babies**
Leotia lubrica Persoon : Fries
(lee-OH-sha LOO-brih-cah)

Slippery as eels! Just *try* to pick one of these mushrooms in damp weather. It will slip and slide away from your grasp as if some jokester knew you were coming and had thoroughly lubricated it with grease. We can see why someone long ago chose the species name *lubrica*. Sometimes a mushroom's scientific name *does* make sense. (At other times, you may feel that you could do a better job of naming mushrooms yourself.)

Yellow jelly babies grow in rich humus in woods and appear very commonly through summer and into the fall. Their caps look like small wads of chewing gum. Once you examine a good color photograph, you will recognize them at first sight in the forest. They are edible, but have a bland flavor. As you'd expect, their texture is like gummy jelly. You may wonder why anyone would bother to eat them, but there's no stopping an experimental and optimistic mushroom cook.

> **In a nutshell:** Small, yellow, slippery, jellylike mushrooms with a cap shaped like a wad of chewing gum.

Cap: ⅜" to ¾" across; yellow to yellow-brown; irregularly lobed and wavy; slippery; feels like jelly. On the underside, no gills or pores; paler color than the cap surface; does not form spores (spores formed on surface of the cap).

Spore print: Produced from the surface of the cap; white.

Stem: ¾" to 3" long, ⅛" to ⅜" thick; slippery; colored like the cap.

Growth habit: On the ground, sometimes in large groups, under both hardwood and conifer trees. July to October.

Edibility: Edible.

Copycats: Green jelly babies *(Leotia viscosa)* have dark green caps.

Tip: Because of its slipperiness, it is easier to harvest this mushroom with scissors.

---

58 Green jelly babies

Leotia viscosa Fries
(lee-OH-sha vis-COE-sah)

As you'd expect from its scientific species name, *viscosa,* this mushroom is very slippery and gelatinous—like its close relative, yellow jelly babies *(Leotia lubrica).* In form, the two species look much alike. But they show obvious color differences: overall yellowish to yellow-orange for yellow jelly babies, and a very unusual deep green to deep blue-green cap with white to orange stem for green jelly babies. Although these differences usually distinguish the two species clearly, their occasional color variations confuse mushroomers, as yellow jelly babies *can* have pale greenish-brown-tinted caps. Sometimes you'll see the entire mushroom colored entirely light green. For more confusion, another species, *L. atrovirens,* has a green cap with a green to pale green stem, but it's smaller in size than green or yellow jelly babies. Nevertheless, with all of these curve balls, most mushroomers find green jelly babies to be very distinctive and hard to confuse with any other species.

> **In a nutshell:** Jellylike and slippery mushrooms with a dark green cap and white, pale yellow, or orange stem, growing in clusters and groups.

Cap: ¼" to ⅜" across; dark green or blue-green; shaped like a wad of chewing gum; slippery and gelatinous. The underside is obscure and does not form spores (spores are formed on top of cap).

Spore print: White.

Stem: ¾" to ¹⁄₁₂" long, ¼" to ½" thick; white, orange, or yellowish.

Growth habit: In clusters and scattered on the ground, sometimes on rotting wood. July through September.

Edibility: Edible.

Copycats: *Leotia lubrica* does not have a dark green cap. *L. atrovirens* is colored green all over.

Tip: As all three *Leotia* species mentioned here are edible, in the kitchen it really doesn't matter if you can't tell them apart.

---

59 ## Pear-shaped puffball
Lycoperdon pyriforme Schaeffer : Persoon
(lie-coe-PER-don pie-rih-FOR-meh)

Many of my friends who gather fine-flavored fungi cut their beginner's teeth on pear-shaped puffballs. This puffball is a prime novice's mushroom because it's so easy to identify and plentiful. In warm, moist summer weather *Lycoperdon pyriforme* blankets rotting stumps by the hundreds. Almost everyone likes this mushroom the first time they try it, if they don't mind the marshmallow-like texture typical of puffballs.

Pear-shaped puffballs really do look like little brown pears with their stem ends attached to the wood. Pick a few specimens and you'll see this shape more clearly, although they may be somewhat deformed from crowding in clusters. Distinctive white rootlike (rhizomorphic) threads at the base often remain attached after you pick the mushrooms. The skin covering the surface of pear-shaped puffballs is smooth, not warty or spiny, like some similar-looking species.

Detail: Small, brown, pear-shaped forms; ⅜" to 1 ¼" high, ¾" to 1 ½" across; often shows little white threadlike strands at the base when picked; smooth brown skin; cream cheese white inside when young, becoming yellow-green and then finally dark olive-brown with age; releases spores through a little hole in the top.

Spore color: Dark olive-brown.

Growth habit: In dense clusters on and around old hardwood logs and stumps. July to November.

Edibility: Good when young, fresh, and pure white inside.

Copycats: With its smooth brown skin, small pear shape, white rootlike threads at the base, hole at the top to release spores when old, and growth on wood, there's little chance that you will confuse it with something else.

Tip: Don't keep pear-shaped puffballs long before you eat them, because they can quickly become bitter tasting even before they discolor internally from age.

---

60 Tough skinned puffball

Scleroderma citrinum Persoon
(scle-roe-DER-mah sih-TREE-num)

Has also been called *Scleroderma aurantium* and *Scleroderma vulgare*.

Just between us, this mushroom is not a puffball. From its rounded form and the way it develops its spores internally, it's easy to think that it's a puffball. But the tough, warty hide and interior that remains hard as the spores ripen and darken are very un-puffball-like features. Many guidebooks list it as a puffball anyway, because in some ways it looks like one. From its identifying features, though, you and I know that it is technically an earthball.

You can find this very common earthball in dry weather when most other fungi wait to grow until the next warm rain. Taking advantage of whatever moisture is available, it likes to grow along the banks of streams and in the damp shade of trees.

Tough skinned puffballs are poisonous, according to most authorities. I know several mushroomers who have had gastrointestinal upset with vomiting from eating them. Yet some older guidebooks report that people (mainly in Europe) have used this strongly flavored and scented fungus as a truffle substitute. The authors of these books suggest that you should eat them only while they are young and white inside; be sure to peel them; use only absolutely fresh specimens; never eat them uncooked; and eat only a small quantity at a time. I know mushroomers who grate a tiny amount of the white interior part of a young tough skinned puffball and add it to dishes for a truffle-like taste and odor. When used in this way, none of my acquaintances have experienced ill effects. Some people may have individual sensitivities to the mushroom, though, so I don't recommend that you try this.

In a nutshell: Round or flattened, ball shaped, with a thick yellow brown warty hide; when ripe, develops an open pore at the top.

Detail: 1" to 4" across; yellow-brown; with a thick warty hide; forms an opening at the top when mature to release the spores.

Spore color: Blackish brown.

Growth habit: Singly, in small groups, or in small clusters on the ground in damp places around trees and logs or under trees.

Edibility: Caution! Can cause gastrointestinal upset with vomiting.

Copycats: *Scleroderma meridionale* grows in sand dunes; *S. areolatum* is thin skinned when mature; *S. flavidum* is smooth skinned when young. There are a few others. All may be toxic.

Tip: If your spirit of curiosity and adventure overwhelms your natural precautions and you decide to add a bit of this earthball to a dish, be sure to follow the recommendations in the "Edible and Non-Edible Mushrooms" section to test your sensitivity.

61 Cauliflower mushroom

Sparassis crispa Wulfen : Fries
(spa-RASS-iss CRISS-pah)

The first time you come upon this mushroom in the woods, you may wonder whether a careless picnicker lost a cauliflower from his or her basket. From a distance, *Sparassis crispa* looks more like the familiar garden vegetable—in size, color, and form—than a fungus. Up close, though, the resemblance ends. Instead of the thick, firm, branching florets of cauliflower, the branches of this mushroom form a mass of thin, flattened, wavy lobes. The frilly fungal shape may remind you of the ruffled collars worn by well-to-do art patrons in paintings from the 1600s.

Cauliflower mushrooms grow from about five inches to two feet across, but the larger sizes are rare in this region. Bringing one of these big, beautiful mushrooms home is a special event for a mushroomer. Connoisseurs everywhere appreciate its fine flavor. Hikers and others who enjoy the beauty of the woods may not appreciate your collecting such a magnificent fungus. When you inform them that it is a parasite of pine trees, though, they may change their attitude.

In a nutshell: Large, round mushroom, resembling a cluster of whitish or yellowish egg noodles.

Detail: 6" to 12" across, and 6" to 10" high; forms a rounded clump of white to yellowish flat, thin, wavy ribbons; rooted with a thin cord.

Spore print: White.

Growth habit: Near pine and sometimes oak trees, on the ground in open woods. July to October.

Edibility: Excellent.

Copycats: *Sparassis herbstii* has larger branches.

Tip: If you dry this mushroom quickly, it will shrink but keep its attractive form. Then it makes an attractive and permanent desktop decoration.

Pored (boletes)

62 Birch bolete

Austroboletus betula (Schweinitz) Horak
(os-troe-boe-LEET-us BET-you-lah)

Also called *Boletellus betula* and *Boletus betula* in some guidebooks.

Like birdwatchers, mushroomers often try to see how many species they can find in an outing or through a season. They especially enjoy spotting rarities or those that are uncommonly found in their region. I include this mushroom because finding it was such a remarkable experience. Many mushroomers in the southern part of this region and along the Atlantic coast are familiar with this species, but it is rare in the central and northern areas. I found it only one time—and as my birdwatcher friends would do, I phoned several local mushroomers and told them about my finding the birch bolete within a few miles of my home. None of them have ever seen it, except in the guidebooks. With global climate change bringing warmer summers, perhaps this species will become more common throughout this region.

It certainly is easy to identify. The long, long stem cut with deep grooves; the distinctly sticky, yellow to reddish brown cap; and the yellow pores that become greenish yellow as they age all distinguish this bolete.

Often you will find a mushroom that you will never see again. Your guidebooks will describe some of these, but even with a lot of investigation, you will not be able to identify others. Don't feel glum. Most guidebooks omit certain rare mushrooms—or you may have found a new species, as yet unknown to scientists.

 In a nutshell: Sticky, yellow-orange cap; yellow pores; long, deeply shaggy, red and yellow stem.

Cap: 1 ¼" to 3" across; orange-yellow; sticky.

Pores: Yellow; not changing color from bruising; becoming green, then more brown, with age.

Spore print: Olive-brown.

Stem: 4" to 8" long; deeply shaggy; red, often with yellow tones.

Growth habit: Scattered on the ground under both hardwood and softwood, mainly in the coastal and southern regions of the eastern United States. August to October.

Edibility: Edible.

Copycats: *Boletellus russellii* has a dry, woolly, yellow-brown cap. It, too, is edible.

Tip: If you have good reason to think that you have found a new mushroom species, you can do some things that could be important to mycology. First, in a notebook, describe the features of the mushroom in great detail. Be sure to include the date, location, and any other information that may be useful. Next, take very good color photographs of the mushroom growing in place—and lots of them. Include close-ups of various views of the mushroom, both external and internal after you slice it in half. Get a good spore print. Finally, carefully dry and preserve several specimens. Contact the author of a recently published good mushroom guidebook and ask where to send your material for examination. While unlikely, it is possible that you will discover a new mushroom species. If you do, there is a tiny chance that it will be named after you.

---

63 **Spotted bolete**
Boletus affinis var. *maculosus* Peck
(boe-LEE-tus a-FINE-nis mack-you-LOE-sus)

Like a clown, this bolete wears a reddish brown cap with pale yellow polka dots. For savvy mushroomers, its exhibitionism invites a one-way trip to the frying pan. Although its edible qualities are rated lower than certain other boletes, the spotted bolete is worth knowing because you can sometimes find lots of it. Young specimens are better for cooking, because the mushroom becomes soft and soggy when it gets old.

Its cap colors make this mushroom easy to identify. To be sure, turn the mushroom over and check the

In a nutshell:

Reddish brown cap with pale yellow dots; whitish pores that develop rusty yellow colors when bruised; smooth stem colored like the cap, but often paler.

underside. You'll find off-white pores that develop rusty yellow stains when bruised. The stem is colored like the cap or paler.

Cap: 2" to 4" across; reddish brown to chestnut color, fading with age.

Pores: Off white; become rusty yellow when bruised.

Spore print: Yellow-brown.

Stem: 1 ½" to 3" long, ⅜" to ¾" thick; colored like the cap or paler; smooth or sometimes with a dusty or powdery look.

Growth habit: On the ground under beech, but can grow under other kinds of trees too. June to September.

Edibility: Edible.

Copycats: *Boletus affinis* var. *affinis* is practically identical to the spotted bolete, but it lacks the spots on the cap. Once you become familiar with the spotted *maculosus* variety, the *affinis* variety is easy to identify. It's also edible.

Tip: Some mushroomers prefer to remove the pore layer and stem and cook them together because their textures are similar. The cap texture is softer and is better cooked alone.

---

64 **Orange cap leccinum**
Leccinum aurantiacum (Bulliard) S. F. Gray
(leck-SYE-num are-ran-TIE-a-come)

Boletus scaber var. *aurantiacus* is the old name.

If you find a bolete with a stem covered with small, rough, projecting scales, you probably have a *Leccinum* species. Technically, the scales are called scabers. Scabers are usually pale when young but develop dark brown or black colors as the mushroom ages. *Leccinum* species also have pale pores that do not bruise blue. On the other hand, if you find a bolete with little dark dots, not scales, on the stem, you probably have a species of *Suillus*. To get a clear picture of the differences in these stem decorations, check the photographs and illustrations in your guidebooks.

I'd be surprised to meet a mushroomer who doesn't love orange cap leccinum. They have a crisp, firm texture and rich flavor; a neat, handsome appearance; and they often grow in large quantities. Bugs are eager to gobble up most boletes as soon as they find them, but we often get a first chance at this one.

This mushroom's scaly stem, reddish brown to orange-brown cap, and association with conifer trees make it easy to recognize. A number of very close look-alikes grow in the same habitats, and it's hard to tell them apart without a microscope. Fortunately, they all seem to be edible, although an occasional mushroomer has reported mild stomach upset.

In a nutshell: Brick orange cap; whitish pores; whitish stem covered with short blackish projecting scales.

Cap: 2" to 8" across; bright to dull brick orange-red; slightly sticky; rough in places. When cut or broken, the white interior slowly bruises wine red, then becomes grayish, and finally black.

Pores: Whitish when young, becoming brownish with age; bruise olive.

Spore print: Yellow brown to cinnamon brown.

Stem: 4" to 6 ½" long, ¾" to 1 ¼" thick; white, becoming black with age; covered with coarse, pale scabers that become black with age.

Growth habit: On the ground under aspen and pine trees. August to September.

Edibility: Very good.

Copycats: Edible *Leccinum insigne* does not grow under pine trees and does not turn wine red before turning black. Other similar-looking leccinums grow under birch trees. Some of these may cause digestive upsets.

Tip: The orange cap leccinum often becomes very dark colored when cooked. Beginning mushroomers may be bothered by this color change, but it does not affect the mushroom's edibility.

65 **Old man of the woods**

Strobilomyces floccopus (Vahl : Fries) Karsten
(stroe-bih-loe-MY-sees flo-COE-pus)

It has been named *Strobilomyces strobilaceus.* Known locally as the ol' man.

Once you get a good look at the old man of the woods, you're not likely to confuse it with any other mushroom. Gray and black tones, along with shaggy, coarse, flattened scales that cover the cap and stem, set it apart. As if you needed further help with identification, distinctive color changes appear when you break open a fresh *Strobilomyces floccopus* and expose the interior flesh to air: though initially whitish, it slowly turns a reddish color before finally becoming black. Life would be a lot easier for mushroomers if other species made themselves as easy to identify. It is much harder to pronounce—or remember—its scientific name than to identify this mushroom.

The old man is low on most mushroomers' edible lists. In some years, though, a few may easily end up in your collecting basket because of their abundance. For best eating, choose young specimens. As they age, like many other boletes, they become soggy and develop poor flavors that remind some people of mothballs.

In a nutshell:

Coarse, shaggy, gray and black scaly cap with gray pores beneath and a woolly, gray stem.

You might think that the old man is one of the homeliest mushrooms you've ever laid your eyes on, with the shaggy, grizzled, and timeworn appearance. But after a season or two, after meeting the species often in the woods, you'll tend to soften your judgment. It then becomes just another old friend.

Cap: 1 ½" to 6" across; pale, covered with large soft, coarse, flattened, gray to black scales; grayish pieces of the veil hang from the edge of the cap.

Pores: Large; at first whitish or gray, becoming darker and almost black with age; where bruised, become red colored, then black.

Stem: 2" to 5" long; dark gray, with a shaggy and woolly surface; exposed flesh turns red, then black.

Growth habit: On the ground in hardwood, pine, or mixed woods. July to August.

Copycats: *Strobilomyces confusus* (which is edible) is very similar, but its cap is covered with smaller, hard, upward-pointing dark scales. Most mushroomers don't notice these differences and think of this species as just another old man of the woods.

Tip: With its drab colors against the dark background of the forest floor, the old man easily escapes a beginning mushroomer's notice. So study a good photograph of this species to set your sights clearly before you head to the woods.

---

66 ### Dotted-stem slippery jack, granulated suillus

Suillus granulatus (Linne : Fries) Kuntze
(soo-ILL-us gran-you-LAY-tus)

Boletus granulatus is the older name.

This mushroom grows almost anywhere evergreen trees grow in the United States. In this region, you will frequently see it on your walks through the forests all the way from late spring into early winter. Summer and early fall offer the best picking. Because it's one of the most common mushrooms in woodland picnic places and campgrounds, visitors often unconsciously walk on it—a painful sight for mushroomers who come along later.

Usually, this species has a neat, clean, and appetizing appearance. Most mushroomers consider it one of the best eating of the slippery jacks. To others, it's simply another bland-tasting mushroom. This wide difference of opinion probably reflects the age of the mushroom when collected. Although crispy and tasty while young, it becomes soggy and somewhat flavorless when old.

You will find this mushroom easy to identify. The white or yellowish stem covered with conspicuous little dots is an important and clear earmark. With good weather, you can fill your basket if you find the right collecting places.

 In a nutshell: Brownish, sticky caps; creamy or pale yellow pore layer; whitish stem, covered with little pinkish or brownish dots.

Cap: 1" to 6" across; brownish to cinnamon colored; sticky when moist; surface skin peels off easily.

Pores: Creamy or whitish when young, becoming dull tan or yellowish with age.

Stem: 1 ½" to 3" long, ⅜" to 1" thick; whitish when young. With age, it becomes yellow at the top and dull cinnamon at the base. Covered with little pinkish to brownish colored dots.

Growth habit: Scattered or clustered under pine, hemlock, and spruce trees. July to October.

Edibility: Good, if you get it at the right stage.

Copycats: *Suillus placidus* has a white cap when young. *S. brevipes* lacks the dots on the stem. Certain similar-looking *Suillus* species have cottony tissue along the edge of the cap when young. No look-alike *Suillus* species are known to be poisonous, but some people may have unpleasant reactions from certain species. Test yourself and peel the caps of those species that permit it.

Tip: Collect this jack when it is young, more or less buttonlike, and firm to the touch. Otherwise, it's not in a prime edible state. Use it as quickly as possible, too. If the pores are dirty yellow colored, the mushroom is too old for best eating.

---

67 Painted suillus, red and yellow suillus
Suillus pictus (Peck) Kuntze
(soo-ILL-us PICK-tus)

Older books list it as *Suillus spraguei* and *Boletinus pictus*.

The painted suillus must love mushroomers, because it makes itself so easy to identify. The color features and growth habit are dead giveaways. Unlike most boletes, its annual visits begin in June, early in the season. You can find it as late as the end of October, but the summer months yield the biggest crops. Hunt this mushroom only under white pine trees, because it does not grow anywhere else. Often, this is one of the first species that a novice learns to identify confidently from among the huge and bewildering array of mushrooms in the *Boletaceae* family.

This is a beautiful mushroom with coarse, red, scaly patches covering the cap and the stem below its ring. Beneath these scales lies yellow flesh that turns pink, then brownish (but never blue), shortly after bruising or cutting. White veil fragments often decorate the edge of the cap. To the touch, the mushroom feels sensous, as if it's covered with a layer of very thin felt.

Cooking turns it black, which some people find unappealing. Don't reject it for the dark color, or you will miss a real mushroom treat. If it really bothers you, consider what my grandmother told me to do when I was a child and eyed something foreboding on the dinner plate: close your eyes and eat it.

Many mushroomers put the painted suillus high on their favorite edible species list. Fortunately, it's one of the most prolific of the boletes in this region. An area with lots of white pines can fill your mushroom basket often through the summer months. Although it's scarcer later in the year, you can often find it in November. You will appreciate the neat, clean growing manner that makes cleanup in the kitchen easy.

> **In a nutshell:**
>
> Cap and stem with red scales over yellow flesh that stains pinkish when cut or broken; yellow pores; cottony ring on stem. Grows only under white pine trees.

Cap: 2" to 3" across; covered with red scales, with the yellow color of the underlying flesh sometimes showing between the scales; flesh is yellow, but bruises pinkish or brownish; sometimes with whitish veil fragments on the cap edge.

Pores: With large openings; yellow in youth, more brown colored in age; bruise brown.

Spore print: Olive-brown.

Stem: 1 ½" to 4 ½" long, ⅜" to 1" thick; colored like the cap below the grayish colored ring, and yellowish above.

Growth habit: On the ground under white pine trees, sometimes growing in large numbers. June to November.

Edibility: Very good.

Copycats: This species stains brown when bruised (never blue, as certain other boletes do), and it is found only under white pine trees. *Suillus cavipes* grows under larch and has a hollow stem.

Tip: Painted suillus picking is a fine sport to combine with a summer family picnic. Because the mushroom is so easy to identify, everyone in the family can join in the hunt without much training. Use it as a ploy to keep the kids, who may think that family picnics are dorky, out of trouble. In this region, public picnic grounds are often located in or near places where white pine trees and this mushroom grow. Be sure to find out if wild mushroom picking is permitted there, or your mushrooms may be very expensive. Look for signs, or ask the ranger or attendant.

---

68 ## Violet-gray bolete

Tylopilus plumbeoviolaceus (Snell and Dick) Singer
(tie-LAH-pill-lus plum-bee-oh-vie-oh-LAY-see-us)

You will meet various kinds of mushroom hunters. Some of these collect only boletes. They may not own a guidebook and they may even scoff at the idea of collecting any other kind of edible wild mushroom. They pick according to general rules: don't eat any bolete that turns blue when bruised, and/or has red or orange pores, and/or tastes unpleasant raw.

Going by these rules, the violet-gray bolete looks like a top choice for the table. It does not turn blue when bruised. The pore layer is definitely not red, brown, or orange, and the mushroom can taste mild when raw. It goes, then, into the basket with the other edibles. But a surprise awaits the unwary collector. It may end up as part of an elaborate and fancy mushroom dish, laboriously prepared and proudly set out as the centerpiece on the family dinner table. Everyone gets a generous steaming, fragrant serving. Someone takes a big forkful—and unceremoniously heads for the kitchen to spit into the sink. The dish tastes incredibly, inedibly bitter.

Only one piece of the violet-gray bolete or one of its close relatives, like the bitter bolete *(Tylopilus felleus),* can spoil an entire dish. Neither species is reported to be poisonous, just intensely bitter. Many mushroomers, like myself, can't easily detect this bitterness when they taste the raw mushroom. But no one has a problem noticing it after the mushroom is cooked. Be sure to learn to identify this mushroom so that you can keep it out of the kitchen. Otherwise, your reputation as a reliable mushroom collector could be tarnished for a long time.

Knowledgeable mushroomers don't feel comfortable picking mushrooms by general guidelines. They feel it's best to identify each mushroom species with certainty. Then they check its reputation from their guidebooks and, if possible, from experienced mush-roomers before they eat it.

In case you wonder, the curious name *plumbeovio-laceus* refers to the colors of the mushroom—leaden gray and violet. It combines *plumbum,* the old name for lead, and *violaceus,* referring to violet.

> **In a nutshell:** Large, bitter-tasting bolete with purplish gray cap and stem when young and pinkish pores.

Cap: 1 ½" to 6" across; violet-gray, becoming more brown with age; bitter taste.

Pores: Brownish pink, becoming darker with age.

Stem: 3" to 4 ½" long; ⅜" to ⅝" across at the top, but some-times thicker at the bottom; violet-gray colored.

Growth habit: On the ground in hardwood forests. June to September.

Edibility: Inedible. Not poisonous, but very bitter.

Copycats: *Tylopilus felleus,* the bitter bolete, lacks purple tints. *T. rubrobrunneus,* also bitter tasting, develops brown stains on bruised pores and generally begins fruiting in July—later than the violet-gray bolete.

Tip: Even insects don't like to eat this mushroom. Perhaps it contains a bug repellent. This summer, I plan to do an experiment. When the mosquitoes are bothering me in the woods, I'll crush a violet-gray bolete and rub it over my skin and clothing. Will it keep the biters away?

Pored (polypores)

69 **Varnish cap**

Ganoderma tsugae Murrill
(ga-noe-DER-ma SOO-gay)

Has been called *Polyporus tsugae,* as well.

When you walk through the hemlock forests of this region you are in a sacred place. You are in the domain of a kind of mushroom that has been revered, even worshipped, by a large part of the world for thousands of years. Everyone notices the large, dark, red, varnished-looking shelflike caps of varnish cap mushrooms growing from rotting logs and stumps. Not everyone knows that the varnish cap's very close relative, *Ganoderma lucidum* (called *reishi, ling zhi,* or *mannetake*), has been used in traditional healing practices in Asian countries as far back as historical records can be traced. Among its many ancient names are "panacea polypore," "the mushroom of immortality," and "the 10,000 year mushroom." These lofty titles reflect the conviction that it cures cancer and many other diseases and promotes longevity, sexual prowess, wisdom, and happiness. Recent scientific studies confirm some of this fungus's health-giving benefits. Many authorities believe that the varnish cap has the same properties as *reishi*.

Varnish caps are quite common in this region. Appropriately, the species name, *tsugae*, is scientific lingo for hemlock, its favorite food. The fan-shaped varnished red caps, smooth white porous undersides, and hard woody texture make identification very easy. The bulk of the mushroom body is much too tough to eat, but the thin, tender growing edges make a very good-tasting dish. I know a number of mushroomers who dry the fungus and grind it into a coarse powder to make a healthful tea.

Some mushroomers avoid eating any mushrooms that grow on hemlock wood. After all, didn't Socrates die from hemlock poisoning? Couldn't mushrooms take up the poison from the wood? Don't worry. The hemlock tree is not poisonous, though the root of another plant named poison hemlock—a relative of the carrot family that grows in moist areas—is extremely toxic. (Anyway, from the detailed historical account of Socrates' death, chances are that he died from puffer fish poisoning.)

> **In a nutshell:**
>
> Big, smooth, shiny, red-varnished, corky fan-shaped cap, with porous whitish underside. Grows on dead hemlock.

Cap: 2" to 12" across; shiny and varnished looking; orange to red, sometimes almost black; soft, but corky. The edge is usually pale and soft.

Pores: White to brown; discolor brownish when bruised; tiny.

Spore print: Light brown.

Stem: Often looks like an extension of the cap; shiny and varnished looking; same color as cap.

Growth habit: On conifers, mainly hemlock; grows year-round.

Edibility: Edible, but too tough to chew, except when very young or, on mature mushrooms, the growing edge.

Copycats: *Ganoderma lucidum* grows on hardwoods.

Tip: Mature varnish caps are corky and not easy to grind for tea. Chop them into smaller pieces with an ax and then run the pieces through a garden mulcher or chipper a few times.

---

70 ### Giant polypore, blackening polypore

Meripilus sumstinei (Murrill) Larsen in Lombard
(mer-IH-pill-lus sum-STI-nee-eye)

Some guidebooks list this species, incorrectly, as *Meripilus giganteus* and as *Polyporus giganteus.*

A mature giant polypore is a spectacular sight. Hikers look like elves when photographed alongside one of these monsters. A mushroomer hunting something for dinner may need help to carry a giant polypore away, because this edible fungus can weigh more than thirty pounds! You will rarely find it that big in this region, but three-pound to ten-pound specimens are common. That's still a lot of mushroom.

At first sight, you may think you have found an early fruiting, overachieving, and overfluffed hen of the woods. Both look like a big, flat, branching undersea coral. But the giant's overlapping caps tend to be larger than the hen's and less crowded, giving it a more open appearance. In this region, it grows as early as June, while the hen typically comes on in August. If you are not sure which species you have, pinch one of the caps. The underside of the giant polypore's cap soon stains blackish from the bruise. The hen of the woods doesn't show a blackish stain.

Young or old, the giant polypore has a fine flavor. Some people prefer it to the famous hen of the woods, but the giant's texture can be tough and leathery. Long, slow cooking helps. The edges of the caps are the most tender part. Mushroomers often trim these away to take home, leaving the rest of the mushroom in place. With age, the caps become tougher and the tender edges become thinner. Old specimens offer only a meager handful of chewable thin trimmings, saving you from overindulging.

In a nutshell: Large open clumps of overlapping, soft, brownish, fan-shaped, black-bruising caps joined to a large stem. Grows at the base of hardwood trees and stumps.

Cap: 2" to 8" across; brownish; fan shaped; covered with fine fuzz; bruise blackish along the edge.

Pores: White, staining blackish when bruised.

Spore print: White.

Stem: Brownish yellow; thick and short, like an obscure extension of the cap.

Growth habit: In large, open, coral-like clumps on the ground around oak stumps and trees. July to September.

Edibility: Good.

Copycats: Not easily confused with other mushrooms. None of its look-alikes turns black when bruised. Edible hen of the woods (*Grifola frondosa*) typically appears later in the season, and its caps are smaller and more crowded. Some guidebooks list this mushroom as *Meripilus giganteus,* but that species probably does not grow in North America.

Tip: Save the tough parts to boil for a fine-flavored soup or gravy stock.

summer mushrooms

14 Weeping psathyrella, *Psathyrella velutina*, p. 52

15 Horse mushroom, *Agaricus arvensis*, p. 53

16   Meadow mushroom, *Agaricus campestris,* p. 55

17   Bracelet cortinarius, *Cortinarius armillatus,* p. 57

18   Sticky violet cort, *Cortinarius iodes,* p. 58

19 Aborted entoloma, *Entoloma abortivum,* p. 60

20 Caesar's mushroom, *Amanita caesarea,* p. 61   *Photo: Joey Korn*

21 Fly mushroom, *Amanita muscaria* var. *Formosa,* p. 63

22   Blusher, *Amanita rubescens,* p. 64

23   Grisette, *Amanita vaginata,* p. 66

24 Destroying angel, *Amanita virosa*, p. 67

25 Wolf asterophora, *Asterophora lycoperdoides*, p. 69

26 Club foot, *Clitocybe clavipes*, p. 70

27 Orange-gilled waxy cap, *Hygrophorus marginatus* var. *concolor*, p. 71

28 False chanterelle, *Hygrophoropsis aurantiaca*, p. 73

29 Common laccaria, *Laccaria laccata*, p. 74

30 Purple-gilled laccaria, *Laccaria ochropurpurea*, p. 76

31 Wrinkled milky, *Lactarius corrugis*, p. 77

32 Blue milk mushroom, *Lactarius indigo*, p. 78

33 Peppery milk mushroom, *Lactarius piperatus* var. *piperatus*, p. 79

34 Wine milk mushroom, *Lactarius subpurpureus*, p. 81

35 Orange-brown lactarius, *Lactarius volemus* var. *volemus*, p. 82

36 American lepiota, *Lepiota americana*, p. 83

37 Parasol mushroom, *Macrolepiota procera*, p. 85

38   Platterfull mushroom, *Megacollybia platyphylla*, p. 86

39   Common mycena, *Mycena galericulata*, p. 87

40   Jack o' lantern, *Omphalotus olearius*, p. 89

41   Rooted xerula, *Xerula radicata*, p. 90

42   Fuzzy foot, *Paxillus atrotomentosus*, p. 92

43   Firm russula, *Russula compacta*, p. 93

44   Crusty russula, *Russula crustosa*, p. 94

45   Fragrant russula, *Russula laurocerasi*, p. 95

46   Variable russula, *Russula variata*, p. 96

47 Green russula, *Russula virescens*, p. 97

48 Vase-shaped puffball, *Calvatia cyathiformis*, p. 99

49 Chanterelle, *Cantharellus cibarius*, p. 100

50 Cinnabar chanterelle, *Cantharellus cinnabarinus,* p. 102

51 Small chanterelle, *Cantharellus minor,* p. 103

52 Golden fairy spindle, *Clavulinopsis fusiformis,* p. 104

53 Horn of plenty, *Craterellus fallax,* p. 105

54 Bird's nest fungus, *Crucibulum laeve,* p. 106

55 Orange jelly, *Dacrymyces palmatus,* p. 108

56 Scaly chanterelle, *Gomphus floccosus,* p. 109

57 Yellow jelly babies, *Leotia lubrica*, p. 110

58 Green jelly babies, *Leotia viscosa*, p. 111

59 Pear-shaped puffball, *Lycoperdon pyriforme*, p. 112

60 Tough skinned puffball, *Scleroderma citrinum*, p. 113

61 Cauliflower mushroom, *Sparassis crispa*, p. 115

62 Birch bolete, *Austroboletus betula*, p. 116

63 Spotted bolete, *Boletus affinis* var. *maculosus*, p. 117

64 Orange cap leccinum, *Leccinum aurantiacum*, p. 118

65 Old man of the woods, *Strobilomyces floccopus*, p. 120

66 Dotted-stem slippery jack, *Suillus granulatus*, p. 121

67 Painted suillus, *Suillus pictus*, p. 122

68 Violet-gray bolete, *Tylopilus plumbeoviolaceus*, p. 124

69 Varnish cap, *Ganoderma tsugae*, p. 125

70 Giant polypore, *Meripilus sumstinei*, p. 127

fall
mushrooms

71 Shaggy mane

Coprinus comatus (Müller : Fries) S. F. Gray
(co-PRY-nus co-MAY-tus)

Known locally as shaggie, shaggy inky cap.

Start looking for this extroverted mushroom around the time of the first fall frosts in this region. It boldly shows itself off in big dense patches of bright white caps against the dark green background of mowed lawns. It seems to beg to be picked. Because it's so easy to see, it's a mushroom you can hunt from your car as you drive around suburban areas. Mushroomers in this region call the technique "road hunting." (While this may be a good method for hunting shaggy manes, puffballs, and certain other species, forget it in morel season. Most mushroomers can't see morels unless they walk right up to them.)

Those beautiful white shaggy mane caps don't last long, especially in warm weather. Like other *Coprinus* species, within a few hours they begin to dissolve into black goo from the bottom of the cap upwards. It's not decay, but a natural self-digesting process that allows the mushroom to propagate itself. That black icky stuff contains millions of spores. Most mushroom species use the wind to disperse their spores, but inky caps rely more on the rain to wash this black material away to spread their spores around. This self-dissolving process can be so fast that the caps can disappear in one day, leaving a bare stem behind. So when you gather shaggy manes for dinner, take the young ones and get them home fast. If you plan to keep them for more than a couple of hours before cooking, store them in ice water.

The shaggy mane is one of the best beginner's mushrooms. It doesn't look much like any other species. Besides being easy to find, it has a wonderful delicate flavor. Practically every mushroom guidebook describes it because it is cherished around the world. For many novices, the first wild mushroom that they eat is the shaggy mane.

In a nutshell: Large, late-season, oblong shaggy white caps that dissolve into black goo. Grows in groups in lawns and grassy places.

Cap: 1 ½" to 3" long; oblong when young, but opening to a bell shape with age; white, soon dissolving into a black sludge; surface covered with yellowish scales, giving it a shaggy appearance.

Gills: White, becoming pinkish or reddish, then dissolving into a black liquid.

Spore print: Black. It's difficult to make a clean print because the gills liquefy quickly.

Stem: 3" to 6" long, ⅜" to ¾" thick; white, smooth, hollow; with a ring when young.

Growth habit: In groups, mostly in lawns, but also in pastures and waste places. Mainly September through October.

Edibility: Excellent.

Copycats: Not easily confused with other mushroom species. Check out other *Coprinus* species in this book and other guides.

Tip: When you clean shaggy manes in your kitchen, expect to trim away lots of inky black gunk. Don't throw it in the garbage pail, though. Scatter it around your lawn and on places where the soil was disturbed or dug up. If you are lucky, you may be picking shaggies in your backyard next fall and probably for years afterward. This is one of the easiest mushrooms to cultivate this way.

Gilled; brown spores

72 **Painted cortinarius**
Cortinarius bolaris Fries
(cor-tin-NAR-ree-us boe-LAR-riss)

This mushroom seems to enjoy playing hide-and-seek. In most places in this region, you can search for a good part of your lifetime and not find it. Little wonder that it's left out of many guidebooks. Then, in a year when the conditions are right, it comes out of hiding with flamboyance and pizzazz. At those rare, special times when you find it, you will wonder how such a shy mushroom can be so gaudy and easy to identify.

A white cobwebby veil stretches between the edge of the cap and stem when the mushroom is young. Small red scales cover the cap and stem. When you handle the painted cortinarius, yellowish red stains appear on the stem from bruising. Too bad more mushrooms don't display such distinctive features. Mushroomers appreciate such cooperation when they set out to identify a new species.

Unfortunately, you will find very few, if any, modern authorities who recommend that you eat this mushroom. That should not come as a surprise, because very few *Cortinarius* species are listed as edible nowadays, no matter what the old guidebooks say.

> **In a nutshell:**
>
> Mushroom with cap and stem decorated with small red scales; stem bruises yellow-red and has a swollen base; pale cinnamon-colored gills when old.

Cap: 1 ¼" to 3" across; whitish or pale tan and covered with small red scales; slightly knobbed in the center; with a thin, white, cobwebby membrane between the cap edge and stem when young.

Gills: Light tan, becoming pale cinnamon color when old.

Spore print: Rusty brown.

Stem: 1 ½" to 2 ⅜ long, ¼" to ⅜" thick; whitish, covered with red scales; stains yellowish red when bruised; often swollen at the base; hollow when old.

Growth habit: On the ground in groups or clusters, under both conifers and hardwoods; often near blueberry and huckleberry bushes. August to October.

Edibility: Unknown. Not recommended.

Copycats: *Tricholoma aurantium* makes a white spore print. *Suillus pictus* has red scales on the cap and stem but has pores, not gills, under the cap.

Tip: The little scales that adorn this mushroom and certain other species are technically called squamules

(SKWAH-mules). This fun word often gets a smile from beginning mushroomers.

---

73 Deadly galerina

Galerina autumnalis (Peck) Smith and Singer
(gal-eh-RYE-na aw-tum-NAL-liss)

Don't let this innocent-looking little brown mushroom fool you. It's just as poisonous as the most deadly *Amanita* species and one of the very few mushrooms in this region that will kill you. As with many of the local very poisonous species, deadly galerinas are very common. They are not conspicuous, but in most years you will find them on your autumn walks if you look for them. All mushroomers should learn to recognize this species to be sure that it will never end up in their basket of edibles.

A beginning mushroomer quickly learns that the woods are full of little brown mushroom species that resemble deadly galerinas. Many of these are extremely difficult to identify. In fact, many are not described in any mushroom guidebook because they have not been named. It's impossible to learn all the mushrooms in your area, then, even if you have a collection of the best guidebooks. (Don't let this information discourage you, though. Nature provides such a large number of identifiable species that you will be busy for many years adding to your mushroom knowledge bank.)

Fortunately, deadly galerinas are distinguishable from other little brown mushroom species if you know to look for certain features. Check the photo and read the description carefully in this book and others. Careless and uninformed psychedelic mushroom hunters are particularly vulnerable, because the species they hunt for are also typically small and brown. Their mistakes can lead to a one-way trip. Beginning velvet stem mushroom *(Flammulina velutipes)* hunters need to be careful, too.

In a nutshell: Small brown mushrooms with thin stems, rusty brown spores, and a thin, delicate ring on the stem. Grows in clusters on rotting wood, mainly in the fall.

Cap: ½" to 1 ½" across; dark brown to yellow brown, but fading to lighter colors as it dries; sticky when moist.

Gills: Attached to the stem; brownish, but becoming darker with age.

Spore print: Rusty brown.

Stem: ¾" to 3" long, ⅛" to ¼" thick; with a thin delicate white ring that can become rusty brown colored on top from the falling spores; with delicate white scales below the ring.

Growth habit: Typically grows in clusters and groups on hardwood and coniferous stumps and logs, mainly in the autumn (October to November). It sometimes can be found in spring and summer.

Edibility: *Deadly poisonous.*

Copycats: Velvet stem mushrooms *(Flammulina velutipes)* have white spores, a dark velvety stem in age, and more orange-to-yellow cap colors. Be careful with any small, brown, wood-growing mushrooms.

Tip: If you are a beginning mushroomer, be sure that you learn to recognize this species. After you know it, teach everyone to recognize it.

Gilled; white spores

74 Honey mushroom

Armillaria mellea (Vahl : Fries) Kummer
(are-mill-LAR-ree-ah MELL-lee-ah)

Some guidebooks list this species as *Armillariella mellea.*
Known locally as stump mushroom, stumpie, honeys, pipinky, pinky.

When the trees show their first flushes of color in late September, mushroomers know that it's time to get a big basket—or perhaps two or three of them—and head for the outdoors. In fact, you may need all the containers you can carry. It's the beginning of honey mushroom hunting season.

For some mushrooms, supply is limited and competition is keen. You can come home with an empty basket after a daylong hunt for morels, for example, unless you are on your toes. Not so for honey mushrooms. Generally, you won't have any trouble finding them, because they are not fussy about where they grow. You can find them at the base of stumps and living trees almost anywhere: on mountainsides, lawns, fields, forests, and picnic areas. In a good season, there's more than enough for everybody. No one will mind your gathering as much as you can carry away, because this fine edible mushroom is a deadly parasite of living trees, including fruit trees. That's why it is not commercially cultivated. We don't need more honey mushroom spores flying around in the air.

Beginners often have trouble identifying honey mushrooms because they tend to be more variable in their appearance than just about any other common mushroom. They come with big smooth yellow caps, small hairy brown caps, and even pinkish colored caps. The gills may run down the stem, simply join to it, or be notched near the stem. The ring on the stem may be white or yellowish. Because of this great variability, authorities call this mushroom a "complex" of species that needs continuing scientific study. As with other mushrooms that are difficult to learn, the best advice is to go slowly. After a time you will be able to identify honeys at a glance.

In a nutshell:

Dense clusters of medium to large brown or yellowish brown mushrooms with white spores growing on or near wood in late fall. The stem has a ring; gills attach to the stem or run down it.

Cap: 1" to 6" across; yellow to some shade of tan or brown; sometimes with blackish-colored scales or hairs.

Gills: White, sometimes slightly yellowish or pale pinkish tan; becoming discolored as they age; attached to the stem or running down it.

Spore print: White.

Stem: 1" to 6" long, ¼" to ¾" thick; tough and stringy; with a ring that may be white or yellowish, cottony or thin and cobwebby—or sometimes disappears altogether.

Growth habit: In dense (often huge) clusters on and around living and dead wood; very common; grows around the world. September to October.

Edibility: All forms are edible and taste like shiitake mushrooms to many people. Be sure to cook them well before you eat them. Don't eat them if you find them growing on horse chestnut wood, because then they can make you sick.

Copycats: Edible *Armillaria tabescens* is a dead ringer for the honey mushroom, except that it lacks a ring on its stem. Deadly poisonous *Galerina autumnalis* is smaller and makes a brown, not white, spore print.

Tip: Foxfire is rotten wood penetrated by honey mushroom mycelium. You may have seen it glowing with an eerie green light in the woods on a dark summer night. Chemical reactions similar to those of fireflies create the illumination.

---

75 ## Sooty hygrophorus

Hygrophorus fuligineus Frost
(hye-GRAH-for-us full-lih-JIN-nee-us)

Known locally as slimy, deer dropping mushroom, deer poo.

Mushrooms can be clever. Like other living creatures, they have some surprising resources when it comes to survival. Since the slimy mushroom grows at the time of fall frosts, it has developed a way to avoid being damaged by the cold: it coats itself with a thick insulating layer of slime. When the temperatures briefly drop below 32°F, this coating freezes and protects the underlying tissue. Their growing season ends when the chilly spells last so long that the freezing temperatures penetrate this barrier.

Slimys are edible, but collecting these slippery mushrooms is a challenge, especially in the button stage. Like watermelon seeds, they easily slip out of your hands—and then land on the forest floor, picking up debris that you will need to clean off. You may start picking slimys with a smile, but soon you may be cursing. Gloves help, but they get gummed up fast. The best way to gather them is to insert your knife deeply into the soil under a slimy and slice through the rooted stem. Then give a little lift with the knife to loosen the mushroom, and use the knife to help move it into your hand. Then you may be able to hold it long enough to clean it and get it into your basket.

Those late fall days are short. Be careful when you gather slimys in dim light, because the little dark buttons look very much like deer droppings. You will know right away if you pick up a deer dropping instead of a slimy. The deer dropping won't slip from your fingers and will easily go into the collecting basket, where it will stick to the mushrooms.

> **In a nutshell:** Very slimy, dark brownish gray to black mushrooms. Grow in very late fall and early winter on the ground under white pine trees.

Cap: 1" to 3" across; very slimy, especially in wet weather; dark brownish gray to black color.

Gills: White; run down the stem.

Spore print: White.

Stem: 2" to 4" long, ⅜" to ¾" thick; very slimy; sometimes with a vague ring or ringlike zone; yellowish above the zone, more colored like the cap below.

Growth habit: In groups under white pine. October and November.

Edibility: Edible, but not very exciting to most mushroomers.

Copycats: *Hygrophorus hypothejus,* which is edible, has a lighter-colored cap that becomes yellowish or reddish in age. Its gills become yellowish with age.

Tip: Take plenty of paper napkins or, better, a large cloth along when you go slimy hunting. If you wipe the gunk and debris from the mushrooms before you put them in your basket, you will have a much, much easier cleaning job back home in the kitchen.

---

76 **Reddish waxy cap**
Hygrophorus russula (Fries) Quélet
(hye-GRAW-for-us RUSS-su-lah)

Pink, plump, and puzzling! This appealing mushroom has caused a lot of confusion for beginners. With its reddish colors and general form, the reddish waxy cap resembles a *Russula* species. Yet you could easily think that you've found a *Tricholoma* species from its large, bulky appearance and white spores. (You'll find it listed as *Tricholoma russula* in older guidebooks.) Once you know the subtle earmarks, the reddish waxy cap is easy to identify. When you rub your fingers over the surface of the gills, they feel waxy, almost like the surface of a candle. *Russulas* and *Tricholomas* do not have this feature, but *Hygrophorus, Hygrocybe,* and certain species of *Laccaria* do. Unlike *Russula* species, the edge of the young caps is delicately fuzzy under magnification. In addition, the cap, gills, and stem of the reddish waxy cap become splotched with reddish stains in age or slowly from bruising.

In many places in this region, years can go by without your finding this handsome mushroom. In a good season, though, it can be plentiful. Although tending to grow in small groups, the size of the individual specimens can be large, even more than five inches across. One find can make a sizeable meal. Look for it under hardwood trees.

Opinions about the flavor vary widely. Most mushroomers think that the reddish waxy cap is a very good eating mushroom. Others think it has a slightly unpleasant, waxy feel in the mouth. Because the quality depends upon preparation, I usually turn them over to a better cook than myself rather than risk botching up the batch.

> **In a nutshell:**
>
> Big, thick, red to pink, sticky caps; white gills with reddish spots; gills attached to a reddish stained white stem and extending down it slightly.

Cap: 2" to 5" across; pale pink to rosy red; firm and fleshy; smooth, sticky when moist, and often dotted with small scales; edge fuzzy when young.

Gills: Attached to the stem and sometimes slightly running down the stem; white, usually slowly becoming red spotted when bruised and with age; somewhat waxy feeling.

Spore print: White.

Stem: 1" to 2" long, ⅝" to 1 ⅜" thick; solid feeling; white or pinkish, with no ring.

Growth habit: Scattered, often clustered; sometimes in fairy rings; on the ground under oak trees. September and October.

Edibility: Good.

Copycats: Certain look-alikes grow under conifer trees, not oak. *Laccaria* species have tougher, stringier stems. *Russula* species do not have a fuzzy-edged cap. *Tricholoma* species do not have waxy-feeling gills.

Tip: The red splotchy spots that this species' gills develop are an important identifying feature.

---

77 ## Smooth lepiota

Lepiota naucinoides Peck
(leh-pee-OH-tah naw-sih-NOY-des)

Mycologists have named this species *Lepiota naucina, Leucoagaricus naucinus,* and *Leucoagaricus naucinoides.* Known locally as white under.

From a mushroomer's point of view, this species seems to have everything going for it. It appears in the colder months of the fall, after most mushroom species have run their season. It's very common and sometimes you can find large quantities of it. It doesn't get bug infested easily. It has a clean, neat, prim, appetizing look. To top it off, it has a delicious flavor. You might think that the smooth lepiota is an ideal mushroom for beginners, right? Wrong.

The problem with the smooth lepiota is its close resemblance to deadly poisonous white species of *Amanita.* All are about the same size, entirely white, have gills that are free from the stem, have rings on the stem, and give a white spore print. This similarity is so close that many mushroomers, even people with years of mushrooming experience, avoid this *Lepiota* species. Considering all the fine edible mushrooms available throughout the year, they feel that they'd rather avoid the risks. Yet some very experienced mushroomers eat it every year—after giving each specimen they pick a thorough examination before they put it in their baskets.

To help you distinguish between smooth lepiotas and local deadly species of white *Amanita,* look for these differences:

- Smooth lepiota gills darken when cooked. *Amanita* gills don't.
- The stem of smooth lepiota typically has a smooth, undecorated bulb at the base. The base of the stem of deadly poisonous local white amanitas is set in a sheath or cuplike structure.
- Smooth lepiotas generally grow in open, grassy places. The local toxic white amanitas tend to prefer woodsy places.

- You can usually move the ring up and down the stem of a smooth lepiota, but the ring does not move easily for *Amanita*.
- The cap and stem of the smooth lepiota separate easily, showing a neat ball and socket pattern. Amanita caps and stems do not come apart so easily, and they tend to tear when separated.

In a nutshell:

Smooth, neat-looking, late-season, lawn-growing white mushrooms with white gills unattached to the stem; a ring on the white stem; a smooth simple swelling at the base of the stem; and a white spore print.

There is another problem with collecting *Lepiota naucinoides* for the table. A few authorities say that it has caused gastrointestinal upsets, although I have not heard of it happening around here, nor have I had any difficulties from eating it almost every year for decades. Either some people are sensitive to this species or there are some inedible varieties of it. Alternatively, there may be very similar-looking inedible species that are not recognized by mushroom authorities yet.

Cap: 2" to 4" across; white and smooth.

Gills: White; free from the stem; becoming pale pinkish brown as the mushroom ages.

Spore print: White.

Stem: 2" to 3" long, ¼" to ⅝" thick; smooth and white; hollow, with a movable ring. The stem base is often shaped like a bulb.

Edibility: Good, but be very cautious with your identification. Avoid eating specimens with a grayish cap or an unpleasant smell. Remember the rumors about its causing stomach upsets.

Growth habit: On the ground in open grassy places, often with *Agaricus campestris,* the "pink under." October.

Copycats: Aside from certain deadly *Amanita* species, the smooth lepiota also resembles the edible meadow mushroom, *Agaricus campestris,* which gives a brown spore print and has pink gills while young.

Tip: Study the differences between this species and poisonous white *Amanita* species in as many mushroom guides as you can find. Learn to identify the smooth lepiota, but put it at the bottom of your list of edible mushrooms for safety's sake.

78 **Orange tricholoma**

Tricholoma aurantium (Schaeffer : Fries) Ricken
(trick-coe-LOE-ma are-RAN-tee-um)

Formerly called *Armillaria aurantia*.

As if proudly signing its name in colored ink, this attractive mushroom often stains your hands bright orange when you handle it, even lightly. In case you wonder whether it's kindly offering you a sign to help you identify another woodland delicacy with ease, smell the mushroom and think again. That odor has been described in many ways, but most mushroomers would agree that one word will suffice: disagreeable. If your inquisitive and skeptical nature needs further proof of its unpleasantness, take a little taste on the tip of your tongue.

Obnoxious though the odor and taste may be, this mushroom is edible, according to many authorities. We have to respect those daring and dedicated mushroomers of the past who overcame all common sense and risked their well-being to prove to the world that we can eat *Tricholoma aurantium* and not be poisoned. I have not tried eating this species.

The orange trich is one of the prettiest mushrooms of the fall woods. Unlike many other fall-growing species, it's not especially common in much of this region. But every year, for more than fifteen years, I have seen it come up in the same places, so it seems to tolerate diverse weather conditions in its season. Wouldn't it be nice if more mushrooms were as adaptable?

In a nutshell: Orange, scaly, sticky caps that often stain the hands orange; white gills; orange, scaly stem, with a white zone at the top; unpleasant odor. Grows on the ground in woods.

Cap: 2" to 2 ¾" across; orange-red; scaly; sticky, often with drops of orange liquid; unpleasant odor.

Gills: White; depressed at the stem; developing rusty brown spots when old.

Spore print: White.

Stem: 1 ½" to 2 ¾" long, ⅜" to ⅝" thick; scaly and orange-red colored, with a white zone at the top.

Growth habit: In groups or scattered on the ground in mixed woods. August to October.

Edibility: Definitely not recommended.

Copycats: *Tricholoma zelleri* is very similar, but has a ring on the stem.

Tip: Be careful not to let this mushroom touch your clothes, because it can leave stains that can be difficult to remove.

---

79 Fragrant armillaria, eastern matsutake
Tricholoma caligatum (Viviani) Ricken complex
(trick-coe-LOE-ma cal-lee-GAY-tum)

Also listed as *Armillaria caligata* in some guidebooks. Known locally as smelly mushroom.

When you first find *Tricholoma caligatum* in this region, you may wonder if you are the victim of some cruel mycological hoax. Most guidebooks tell you that this mushroom is edible and delectable. Some even go into raptures about its wonderful flavor. But it takes only one whiff to doubt the seriousness or sanity of the writers, because this mushroom smells downright awful. A good description of the odor is a blend of rotten cheese and old socks. Yet guidebooks say that you can find varieties of this species with an appealing, sweet scent. I don't know of anyone in this region who has found a good-smelling specimen. Either those pleasantly fragrant varieties don't grow around here or are rare in this region.

Even with its somewhat disgusting aroma, this mushroom is edible. The texture is wonderful and the flavor can be superb. Thank goodness that much of the smell dissipates in cooking. Like other foods with strong peculiar odors—such as garlic, certain cheeses, and some seafood—it can take some time to learn to enjoy this mushroom. The challenge is getting it past your nose. Although I have eaten it several times, I'm still working on making it easy.

This big, bulky species often grows in sizeable groups. One or two patches will fill your basket. With luck, you will come upon a sweet-smelling variety that

In a nutshell:

Big caps with brownish scales; white gills; a thick stem, white above the ring and scaly brown, like the cap, below; sweet or unpleasant smelling. Grows under oaks and sometimes other hardwood trees.

is especially fine eating. Remember where you find fragrant armillarias growing, because they tend to appear in the same places every year.

Cap: 2" to 5" across; covered with dark brown, hairy scales.

Gills: White; close; attached to stem.

Spore print: White.

Stem: 2" to 4" long, ¾" to 1 ¼" thick; with a ring that is white on top and brown beneath; stem white above ring and scaly brown, like the cap, below the ring.

Growth habit: In groups, on the ground, mainly under oak trees. Late September to November.

Edibility: Edible for the adventurous.

Copycats: *Armillaria ponderosa,* also edible, is larger, all white, and stains brown when cut or bruised. It has a pleasant odor.

Tip: Be sure to open the windows of your car when you drive home with your basket of *Tricholoma caligatum* for dinner. The odors can build up in such an enclosed place and spoil your appetite.

---

80 ## Man on horseback, canary mushroom
Tricholoma flavovirens (Persoon : Fries) Lundell
(trick-coe-LOE-ma flay-voe-VIE-rens)

Also known as *Tricholoma equestre.*

Why this beautiful species is not more popular with mushroomers, at least in this area, has always been a mystery to me. Its bright yellow color is especially appealing and the flavor is marvelous. One dish of lightly sautéed canary mushrooms should be enough to send you to the woods every autumn with your collecting basket.

I give it a prime position in my list of choice mushrooms. Because it's relatively easy to identify, it's a good mushroom for beginners—but check the comments below on copycats. The golden cap makes it easy to spot, although sometimes it plays peek-a-boo under little mounds of pine needles. In a moist season, it's very common here. In addition, it can grow late into the autumn, when wild mushroom pickings are beginning to get slim. Here's another mushroom with much to offer, but with few collectors. (So much the better for you and me.)

Another one of the mysteries of mushrooming is why this species is called the man on horseback. Perhaps it got the name because some people thought that it was fun to hunt it from horseback; perhaps in the distant past, equestrians wore yellow hats. We could speculate forever.

In a nutshell: Sticky yellow cap that's brownish at the center; beautiful yellow gills, depressed at the junction with the stem; yellowish white stem. Grows under pine trees in the fall.

Cap: 2" to 4" across; yellow, brownish at center, brighter near the edge of the cap; sticky.

Gills: Bright sulfur yellow, with a deep groove or notch near the stem.

Spore print: White.

Stem: Short, fat, and solid; yellowish white.

Growth habit: On the ground in pine forests and in sandy areas of scrubby pine trees. September to November.

Edibility: Excellent.

Copycats: The possibly poisonous *Tricholoma sejunctum* has blackish fibrous streaks at the center of the cap and white or pale yellowish gills. *T. sulphureum* smells disgusting. The edible *T. leucophyllum* has white gills.

Tip: Because this species likes to grow in sandy soil, be sure to wash it very well before you cook it. There's nothing like a mouthful of gritty sand to spoil an otherwise delectable dish.

---

81 **Mouse mushroom**
Tricholoma myomyces (Persoon : Fries) Lange
(trick-coe-LOE-ma my-oh-MY-sees)

It doesn't take much imagination to see the mouselike features of this small mushroom. Mouse-gray fur covers the cap. Its drab color and tendency to grow close to the ground suggest that it's trying to be inconspicuous. Take a specimen in your hand and you are likely to feel that you are holding a little rodent. For folks who don't like mice, the experience can be a bit creepy. For the rest of us, it confirms that mushrooms are endlessly fascinating.

In a nutshell:

Small; dry, mouse-gray, furry cap; whitish gills; smooth whitish stem. Grows under conifer trees.

Some mushroomers enjoy eating mouse mushrooms, but it's a risky business. They represent a "complex," a group of closely related species. Some of these are not identified yet. We need further study to know if they are all safe to eat. Mouse mushrooms also resemble certain poisonous *Tricholoma* species.

Cap: ¾" to 2" across; covered with a mouse-gray fur; cobwebby strands extend from the edge of the cap to the stem when young.

Gills: White; attached to the stem and often depressed near the stem.

Spore print: White.

Stem: ¾" to 2" long, ⅛" to ⅜" thick; white to gray.

Growth habit: Densely scattered on the ground, under conifer trees. September to October.

Edibility: Edible, but very risky!

Copycats: *Tricholoma terreum* lacks the cobwebby cap-to-stem strands. Raw *T. virgatum* tastes hot. There are many other look-alikes—and all are best avoided.

Tip: Be especially careful if you plan to eat gray-capped or brown-capped, white-spored mushrooms with whitish gills. They may be poisonous *Tricholoma* species.

---

82 ## Sooty gray trich

Tricholoma portentosum (Fries : Fries) Quélet
(trick-coe-LOE-ma por-ten-TOE-sum)

Known locally as snow mushroom.

Right off, I want to say that this exceptionally delicious mushroom is definitely not for beginners. It's too easy to confuse it with several other inedible and dangerously poisonous species. If you take the time to learn to identify it positively, however, you can join other serious and careful mushroomers and enjoy its rich, hearty flavor every fall. You will especially appreciate the crisp and crunchy texture that survives through cooking. Knowing that such a choice mushroom awaits you may tempt you to breeze through your guidebooks for a quick identification just before going out and attempting to gather it for dinner. Shortcutting this way can put you in the hospital for several unpleasant days if you make a mistake. Go slowly. This trich can be tricky.

Differences between *T. portentosum* and certain other species can be disturbingly subtle. One of its important distinguishing features is a moist, sticky cap surface. Yet in dry weather, the cap can become completely dry. Another typical feature is the pale yellowish tint of its gills and stem. These colors are virtually invisible in the yellow tone of incandescent lights, so do your identification work in daylight or cool fluorescent light—and remember that you can often find specimens without these yellow colors. You need to become very familiar with the overall personality of this mushroom to identify it with certainty. Such intimacy comes from attention to its details over time. Carefully check its descriptive features below and read about it in as many guidebooks as you can find. Study it in its natural habitat for a few seasons before you invite it home to dinner.

Because it appears so late in the season—or perhaps from natural resistance—it's often insect free. You can frequently find this species in huge quantities in this region. Look for it under white pine trees.

In a nutshell: Sticky gray cap, often with purplish and/or yellowish tints, with thin fibrous skin radiating from the center of the cap; whitish gills, often with yellowish tints; white stem, often with yellowish tints. Grows under pine trees around the time of the first fall frosts.

Cap: 1 ½" to 4 ¾" across; pale gray, often with purplish and/or yellowish tints; with fibrous streaks running outward from the center of the cap; sticky when moist; edge often upturned when mature.

Gills: White, with a peculiar gray and often yellowish tinge; depressed at the stem.

Spore print: White.

Stem: 2" to 4" long, ¾" to 1" thick; white, often tinged with pale yellow.

Growth habit: Singly or scattered on the ground under white pine trees. October.

Edibility: Excellent, but be very careful.

Copycats: A number of gray-capped tricholomas, such as *Tricholoma pardinum,* are poisonous. Discussion of all the look-alikes is beyond the scope of this book.

Tip: Be sure to look beneath the humps in pine needle beds. This mushroom often develops beneath the ground surface material before it breaks through.

Neither gilled nor pored

83 ### Giant puffball, moon melon
Langermannia gigantea (Batsch : Persoon) Rostkovius
(lan-ger-MAN-nee-ah gye-GAN-tee-ah)

Certain guidebook authors call this puffball *Calvatia gigantea, Lycoperdon giganteum,* and *Calvatia maxima.*

You can easily overlook giant puffballs because they camouflage themselves as clean white softballs or soccer balls. They even like to grow in the places where people are likely to play ball: backyards, mowed lawns, fields, and pastures. Although it's easy to spot this mushroom from a couple of hundred feet away, even from a moving car, you need a close-up look to be sure that you are seeing a mushroom and not a piece of athletic equipment.

Mushrooms make a lot of spores. They hitchhike around the world in atmospheric winds, but only a tiny percentage will find suitable places to grow. Some years ago, a mushroom scientist determined that a good-sized giant puffball releases about seven trillion spores. (No, he didn't count them. He calculated.) We can be thankful that most of these spores do not germinate and give rise to more puffballs. Otherwise, we would all be up to our hips in mushrooms in a year. In no time, the fun would go out of mushroom hunting.

You can find giant puffballs up to bushel-basket size. Sometimes they grow in huge circles. You'll never forget the experience of discovering one of these giant snow-white fairy rings. It makes you feel like one of the seven dwarfs.

> **In a nutshell:** A very large, smooth, white, roundish ball shape, with a feel of soft leather gloves when you touch the surface skin.

Detail: Round in shape; from about 8" up to perhaps 30" in size; white, covered with a kid-leather-glove kind of skin; internal tissue is white when young, with a texture that suggests cream cheese; becoming a powdery brown mass from the spores when mature.

Growth habit: Open places, often near the edge of woods, sometimes in large groups. August to October.

Edibility: Excellent. Do not eat it if the interior is not cream cheese white.

Copycats: While many other puffball species grow in this region, the huge size and smooth white skin distinguish the giant puffball. It's not easily confused with other mushrooms.

Tip: Raw or cooked, this is a fine edible mushroom. Because of its large size, it's hard for a family to consume it all before it goes bad. You can avoid this waste by cutting off only what you need from the living mushroom and leaving the rest in place where it is growing. Cutting stunts its development, so you can return a number of times and gather more of the fresh mushroom as you need it.

---

84 Comb coral mushroom

Hericium coralloides (Scopoli : Fries) S. F. Gray
(her-RISS-see-um cor-ra-LOY-des)

You may feel that you are snorkeling at a tropical reef when you first see this magnificent mushroom, because it really does look like an undersea coral. Many mushroomers would vote the comb coral to be the most beautiful fungus that the woods have to offer. And though an especially attractive mushroom is often inedible, this species tastes as good as it looks. (Some think that the flavor resembles lobster.) Anyone can enjoy this delicacy, because *Hericium coralloides* doesn't look much like any mushroom you shouldn't eat.

Be prepared for an adventurous romp through your guidebooks when you sit down to learn about the comb coral. You'd think that the authorities would have gotten the name of such an attention-grabbing species under control long ago. Older mushroom books list it as *Hydnum ramosum*. Certain recent guidebooks name the species *Hericium coralloides,* although tufts at the ends of the branches technically distinguish this species. Some call it *H. laciniatum.* To most mushroomers I know, it's *H. ramosum*. Most authorities tell you that the comb coral mushroom is pure white when young and fresh, and that *H. albietis,* found on the West Coast, can be pink. Pink forms of comb coral frequently appear in the central part of this region, however. And so it goes. Little wonder that some guidebooks have not bothered to include this species.

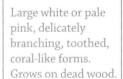

In a nutshell:

Large white or pale pink, delicately branching, toothed, coral-like forms. Grows on dead wood.

Detail:	Up to 10" white or pinkish delicate clusters of tooth-covered branches.
Spore print:	White.
Growth habit:	On decaying hardwood logs and stumps. August to October.
Edibility:	Excellent.
Copycats:	Edible and delicious *Hericium erinaceus* has long, downward pointing teeth.
Tip:	The comb coral mushroom is best for eating when young.

Pored (boletes)

85 American suillus, American slippery jack

Suillus americanus (Peck) Snell
(soo-ILL-us a-mare-ree-CAN-nus)

Formerly called *Boletus americanus*.

I've met two kinds of mushroomers: those who enjoy the flavor of American slippery jack and those who do not. Mushroomers who like to eat it appreciate its okra-like feel in the mouth. Those who leave it in the woods feel that it's too slippery to enjoy. If you have a taste for exotic foods, you will probably like this species.

Through the summer and fall months, the American suillus often produces prodigious mushroom crops. Sometimes you can find it in times of drier weather when many other species won't grow. It only appears under white pine trees, so don't bother to look for it elsewhere. Often you will find it growing in dense lines and arcs that remind you of sections of fairy rings. When you collect the mushrooms, your hands can become covered with sticky yellow goo, especially in wet weather. It's a good idea to take along a bottle of water and a cloth to clean up.

You shouldn't have much trouble identifying this mushroom. With its slimy yellow cap marked with reddish streaks or spots, along with its yellow pores and distinctive red-dotted stem, there is not much else with which you can confuse it.

In a nutshell: Sticky yellow caps with red streaks; yellow pores; reddish brown speckles on stem.

Cap: 1" to 4" across; bright yellow with reddish spots or streaks; sticky; interior flesh is yellow, but turns pinkish or light wine color with exposure to air. Like cottony scraps, remnants of the veil hang from the cap's edge.

Pores: Yellow, becoming more brownish with age.

Spore print: Dull cinnamon.

Stem: 1 ¼" to 3 ½" long and not very fat (⅛" to about ½" thick), often with a slight ring; usually bruises brown from handling; covered with little reddish brown dots.

Growth habit: On the ground under white pine trees. July to October.

Edibility: Edible.

Copycats: In eastern North America, there are no really close look-alikes.

Tip: If you wrap each sticky mushroom in wax paper before you put it in your collecting basket, cleaning will be easier in the kitchen.

---

86 | **Larch slippery jack**
Suillus grevillei (Klotzsch : Fries) Singer
(soo-ILL-us gre-VILL-lee-eye)

This mushroom has also been called *Suillus elegans,* as well as *Boletus elegans.*

When you hunt for honey mushrooms, be sure to check the ground under larch or tamarack trees for larch slippery jacks. Both mushrooms like the same weather conditions and they often grow at the same time. Honey mushrooms, however, appear plentifully for only a few weeks in this region, from late September through October. But you can find larch slippery jacks from September well into November if conditions are favorable.

Larch slippery jacks look neat and colorful. It's hard for anyone to ignore this species. When your friends learn that you are a mushroomer, expect to get their phone calls in the fall asking you to check out the beautiful mushrooms growing in their backyards. Often, they will show you a big crop of larch slippery jacks. In their season, these jacks can be so plentiful that it's difficult to walk under larch trees without stepping on them. When you go hunting for this mushroom, you can easily overfill your basket (and your belly afterward).

Larch slippery jacks have great eye appeal, but it may take you some time to appreciate their mild flavor and soft texture. Be aware that some people have gastrointestinal upsets if they eat the mushroom without first peeling the slimy layer off the cap. I have eaten it unpeeled several times with no problem, but now I always peel it first. Europeans like to pickle this mushroom. Gourmet food stores and supermarkets often have jars of imported pickled slippery jacks.

> **In a nutshell:** Attractive bright yellow to orange-yellow slimy mushroom with bright yellow pores. Grows under larch or tamarack trees.

Cap: 1 ¼" to 6" across; slimy or sticky; shiny; color usually bright orange-yellow here, but may run into reddish brown.

Pores: Bright yellow when young, but becoming olive yellow to dirty brown with age; bruise brownish.

Spore print: Olive brown to cinnamon colored.

Stem: 1 ½" to 4" long, ½" to 1 ¼" thick; pale yellow with chestnut mottling; bruises brownish; with a cottony ring.

Growth habit: On the ground under larch or tamarack trees.

Edibility: Edible—but peel the cap before cooking.

Copycats: Other slippery jack species in this region do not have the combined features of a bright yellow or orange-yellow cap and a preference for larch trees.

Tip: When you are hunting larch slippery jacks, be sure to check around the drip line of the larch tree (at the outermost reaches of the branches). This mushroom often prefers to grow there and can be overlooked.

---

87 Slippery jack
Suillus luteus (Linne : Fries) S. F. Gray
(soo-ILL-us LOO-tee-us)

Has also been called *Boletus luteus*.

Slippery jacks have a plump, neat, and friendly look. This is another mushroom that artists love to illustrate for children's books and romantic fairy tales. They're not so romantic when you handle them, because the caps are unpleasantly sticky and slimy, especially in wet weather. A love-struck prince wouldn't dare offer such a gift to a princess. Few mushroomers are princes or princesses, though, and they would be delighted to receive such a present—slimy or not.

Even with all their gluey gooeyness, slippery jacks are quite good to eat. Just remember to peel the caps first. The slimy layer comes off almost like a thin banana skin, leaving a clean, non-sticky surface on the mushroom. The slimy skin can produce a laxative effect in some people who are sensitive to it. Other mushroomers can eat them unpeeled with no problem, as I have.

When I find slippery jacks, I know that I am into the fall mushroom season, which is many mushroomers' favorite time of the year. You won't find as many species growing then as in the summer. Nevertheless, certain late mushrooms—such as the honey mushroom and slippery jack—often appear in great numbers. Some of the largest species appear late in the year, too: a giant puffball or a large hen of the woods can fill a bushel basket.

> **In a nutshell:**
>
> Slimy brown caps; yellow pores; stem with little dots near the top and with a purplish ring. Grows under pine trees.

Cap: 2" to nearly 5" across; slimy in wet weather; some shade of brown.

Pores: Yellow, developing little dots with age.

Spore print: Dull cinnamon.

Stem: 1 ¼" to 3 ¼" long, ⅜" to 1" thick; little brown dots on the upper part; with a cobwebby veil when young; developing a dark purplish ring in age.

Growth habit: Scattered on the ground under pines and spruce. September into December.

Edibility: Good. Remember to peel the caps before cooking.

Copycats: No very close look-alikes, if you pay attention to the descriptive details.

Tip: Take along wax paper when you are hunting slippery jacks to save clean-up time in the kitchen. As soon as you pick a mushroom, wrap it in the paper. Otherwise, the sticky cap can pick up all kinds of debris.

Pored (polypores)

88 Hen of the woods

Grifola frondosa (Dickson : Fries) S. F. Gray
(grih-FOE-la fron-DOE-sah)

Older books list this species as *Polyporus frondosus*. Known locally as hen.

If you hike in the oak forests in this region in autumn, you probably walk by many hen of the woods mushrooms, but unless you look closely, you may not notice them because of their camouflage. From a distance—even to experienced mushroomers—the mushroom can look like a pile of old leaves against a stump or the base of a tree. If you look more closely, it may remind you of a nesting brownish gray hen, blending in with the surroundings. Yet when you pick the mushroom and turn it around in your hands, it may bring to mind a lump of branching coral from an ocean reef.

Hens are big mushrooms. In this area they grow from double-fist size up to the range of large pumpkins. A typical size is about a foot across; the biggest one I've seen weighed forty-two pounds. When the weather is favorable, lots of hens can grow. So when you go hunting for them, leave your mushroom basket at home. Instead, take a couple of bushel baskets.

Mushroomers around the world eagerly hunt this mushroom. It has a firm, crunchy texture and a rich, meaty, even nutty flavor. On the first taste, you may think that you have never eaten anything comparable. Competition for this species can be intense in some places. Fortunately, oak forests (its favorite habitat) cover much of this region and give mushroomers here plenty of hunting places.

Recent scientific investigations confirm the ancient Asian belief that the hen of the woods mushroom offers a wide range of health-

> **In a nutshell:**
>
> Gray to brown coral-like branching clumps of flat, fan-shaped caps with white porous undersides. Grows at the base of oak trees and stumps.

giving benefits. Health food stores carry a variety of *Grifola frondosa* products, but you will probably see them under the Japanese name *maitake.*

Cap: Caps are about ¾" to 2 ½" across, thin, fan shaped, and colored from gray to brown. Each mushroom has many overlapping caps branching from the main stem.

Pores: White.

Spore print: White.

Stem: White, thick, and short.

Growth habit: On the ground at the base of oak trees and stumps in this area. Guidebooks say, however, that it can be found growing with other hardwoods. September to November.

Edibility: Excellent.

Copycats: The even bigger black-staining polypore, *Meripilus sumstinei,* appears earlier in the year. Unlike hen of the woods, it stains black or gray when bruised. Some mushroomers think that its tender edges are even more delicious than the hen. *Grifola umbellata,* the edible umbrella mushroom, forms branches of cap- and stem-shaped structures. It's rare in this area.

Tip: You will likely find more hens growing with oak trees in parks, picnic grounds, and open public places than you will in the dense woods. Either the mushroom prefers these places or we simply miss seeing them in the forest.

---

89 Chicken mushroom, sulfur mushroom, sulfur shelf

Laetiporus sulphureus (Bulliard : Fries) Murrill
(lay-TIP-por-rus sul-FURE-ree-us)

Polyporus sulphureus and *Grifola sulphureus* are other names that have been applied to this mushroom. Known locally as chicken.

If you like chicken, you will enjoy eating chicken mushrooms because they can taste convincingly like breast meat. Although the basic flavor is delicately mushroomy, a skillful cook will make you believe that you are eating real old-fashioned Kentucky fried. To "pullet off," you may need to practice with the mushroom in the kitchen. You will be surprised at how often you can successfully substitute it for the fowl in chicken recipes. You need to find it at the right stage of development: mature, but not tough and woody from age.

Chicken mushrooms are polypores with tiny pores instead of gills beneath the cap. They are spectacular with their brilliant orange tops and glowing sulfur yellow undersides. Whether you are walking, bicycling, or driving, their flashy colors make them easy to spot from a distance. Growing on trees, stumps, and logs, they form clusters of overlapping shelflike forms sometimes weighing more than fifty pounds. Be prepared for competition—not only from other mushroomers but also from insects and wild animals, such as deer, that love them as much as you do. When you find a nice young cluster, don't go away and wait for the mushrooms to grow larger. Harvest them while you can.

Fortunately, this mushroom is very common in this region. If you spend much time in the outdoors through the summer and fall, you will probably find it. It's not particular about where it grows, either. You can find it just about anywhere, in the deep woods, your backyard, and along the city streets on stumps and wounds in trees.

In a nutshell: Overlapping bright orange fan- or shelf-shaped caps with bright yellow non-gilled undersides. Grows on wood.

Cap: Up to 12" across, bright orange, in overlapping shelf or fan shapes.

Pores: Bright sulfur yellow.

Spore print: White.

Stem: None, or like an extension of the cap.

Growth habit: On dead and living hardwood and softwood trees, sometimes in huge clumps, on logs and stumps. June into early November.

Edibility: Excellent, but can be hard to digest when old and woody. Use young specimens for the table.

Copycats: This is a very easy mushroom to identify and is not easily confused with other species. The edible and closely related *Laetiporus cincinnatus* has a salmon pink cap and white pores. *L. cincinnatus* confuses many beginning mushroomers, however, because it is absent from some mushroom guidebooks. It tends to appear earlier in the season here than *L. sulphureus*. While some mushroom writers call it rare, *L. semialbinus* is very common in this area.

Tip: Remember where you find chicken mushrooms growing, because they can reappear every year, sometimes for several years. If you can carry off the log on which they're growing, put it in your backyard and water it in dry weather. You could be harvesting chickens next summer.

fall mushrooms

71 Shaggy mane, *Coprinus comatus*, p. 152

72 Painted cortinarius, *Cortinarius bolaris*, p. 153

73 Deadly galerina, *Galerina autumnalis* var. *autumnalis,* p. 155

74 Honey mushroom, *Armillaria mellea,* p. 156

75 Sooty hygrophorus, *Hygrophorus fuligineus,* p. 158

76 Reddish waxycap, *Hygrophorus russula,* p. 159

77 Smooth lepiota, *Lepiota naucinoides,* p. 161

78 Orange tricholoma, *Tricholoma aurantium,* p. 163

79 Fragrant armillaria, *Tricholoma caligatum*, p. 164

80 Man on horseback, *Tricholoma flavovirens*, p. 165

81 Mouse mushroom, *Tricholoma myomyces*, p. 166

82 Sooty gray trich, *Tricholoma portentosum*, p. 167

83 Giant puffball, *Langermannia gigantea*, p. 169

84 Comb coral mushroom, *Hericium coralloides*, p. 170   Photo: *Tony Sanfilippo*

85 American suillus, *Suillus americanus*, p. 172

86 Larch slippery jack, *Suillus grevillei*, p. 173

87 Slippery jack, *Suillus luteus*, p. 174

88 Hen of the woods, *Grifola frondosa*, p. 176

89 Chicken mushroom, *Laetiporus sulphureus,* p. 177

winter
mushrooms

90   **Common inky cap**
Coprinus atramentarius (Bulliard : Fries) Fries
(co-PRY-nus a-tra-men-TA-ree-us)

Known locally as alcohol inky.

Don't drink any alcoholic beverages around the time that you eat this inky cap! It contains chemicals that can temporarily make you sick. Pharmacologists have studied this mushroom and come up with medications to help cure alcohol addiction. A person takes the prescribed dosage before a situation in which he or she may be tempted to drink alcohol. The individual will get sick if he or she ingests anything containing alcohol during the time that the drug is active. Eventually, some people following this treatment begin to associate nausea and sickness with alcoholic beverages and lose the desire to drink.

With that warning in mind, this is a good edible mushroom. You just have to remember not to drink alcohol from several hours before to several hours after you eat it, although sensitivity to the disturbing effects seems to vary from person to person. (Leave the wine bottle in the cabinet well before and after the meal.)

I'm always pleased when I find a dense cluster of common inky caps growing in the grass. They remind me of a nest of gray eggs left there by the Easter bunny for a mushroomer to find. With the right weather conditions, you can find big patches of this mushroom from early spring to late fall and on into early winter. If you plan to take them home for cooking, don't waste time. It doesn't take long for the caps to naturally dissolve into black inky goo. That's why they call 'em inky caps.

In a nutshell: Gray-brown cap color, the size and shape of hen's eggs when young; grows commonly in grassy places in clusters; smears your hands with a black goo if you handle older specimens.

Cap: 2" to 3" across as it expands; the size and shape of hen's eggs when young; grayish brown; with fine radial lines near edge of cap; edge of cap and gills dissolving into black mush with age.

Gills: White; very close together when young; becoming black and gooey with age.

Spore print: Black and gooey.

Stem: 3" to 6" long; slender; white; hollow; smooth.

Growth habit: Scattered or in dense clusters in lawns, gardens, and rich soil. Early May to November.

Edibility: Good. Even in its black, gooey, sludgy stage, you can safely eat this mushroom if it is fresh and has not spoiled from bacterial or fungal contamination. Your friends, though, may wonder whether your fungal fervor has pushed you over the edge.

Copycats: It is not easily confused with other species, but do not eat specimens that are growing on wood. They may be *Coprinus insignis,* which is poisonous to some people. The edible mica cap *(C. micaceus)* is much smaller and light brown.

Tip: In times past, we used this mushroom to make ink. You can do it too. Just let a few mushrooms sit at room temperature in a small dish for a day or two, until they collapse into a black paste. Then stir this goo into some water and strain it through a sieve. Now it's ready to use as ink. If you want to keep it, you must add a preservative, such as sodium benzoate.

Gilled; brown spores

91 Scaly pholiota
Pholiota squarrosa (Fries) Kummer
(foe-lee-OH-tah skwah-ROE-sah)

Following the information in older mushroom books, I had, like many other mushroomers, eaten scaly pholiota for years and enjoyed its sweet, earthy flavor. Then newer books came out, warning that the mushroom is mildly poisonous for many people and can give you stomach upset if you happen to be sensitive to it. Fortunately, I am not, nor have I met any mushroomer who is. To be safe, though, I have scratched it off my list of edibles.

The scaly pholiota is a beautiful late fall and winter species that hikers admire and mushroom photographers adore. It certainly is conspicuous, with its covering of dark scales on the cap and stem, a yellowish brown cap, and the habit of sometimes growing in huge clusters in the winter woods.

When boiled, it gives a strong yellowish color to the water, so this species and many others have been used for thousands of years to dye fabrics. While the colors of materials dyed this way are typically dull, mushrooms do offer a wide range of soft, earthy pastel tones. Some mushroomers' primary interest lies in using them to dye clothing that they make by hand.

> **In a nutshell:**
>
> Yellowish brown caps with a garlicky odor; stems covered with dark downturned scales and with a ring; brownish gills. Grows in dense clusters at the base of stumps.

Cap: 3" to 5" across; yellowish brown or paler; dry to the touch; covered with dark upturned scales; yellow internal flesh.

Gills: Attached to stem; pale olive colored when young, turning rusty colored with age.

Spore print: Brown.

Stem: Short, but becomes longer with age; with a ring; scaly below the ring.

Growth habit: Grows in large clusters mainly at the base of both deciduous and evergreen stumps. July to November.

Edibility: Risky.

Copycats: Its garlicky odor and distinctive appearance make it easy to identify. The edible sharp-scaly pholiota (*Pholiota squarrosoides*) has a sticky cap covered with sharp pointed scales.

Tip: Natural clusters of this mushroom would make beautiful centerpieces for the table if they could be kept fresh. Like most other mushrooms, the scaly pholiota quickly deteriorates. You can try freeze-drying an attractive display to preserve it. To do this, you simply place the mushrooms in an open container in your frost-free freezer for some weeks. Eventually the frozen mushrooms will dry out but retain their original fresh appearance. Because they are free of moisture, they will not decay when they are removed from the freezer, unless the atmosphere is humid.

Gilled; purple spores

92 ### Brick top

Hypholoma sublateritium (Fries) Quélet
(hye-foe-LOE-ma sub-la-ter-IT-ee-um)

Also known as *Naematoloma sublateritium.*

If we had beauty contests for mushrooms, the brick top would be a serious contender. Its prim and pretty brick-red caps decorate hardwood stumps and logs through the fall and into the winter. Hikers, mushroomers, and artists love them. You will often see them illustrated in romantic literature, fairy tales, and children's books, along with fly mushrooms and a few other charming species. Most people have seen brick tops but only knowledgeable mushroomers can call them by name. Only mushroomers know how good they are to eat.

If you gather brick tops before the fall frosts, you may be disappointed, because they sometimes have a bitter flavor. Those that grow after frost almost always taste pleasant, however. Many mushroomers believe that insects cause the bitterness problem with the earlier ones. Bugs love them and will often beat you to the harvest. Their mushroom visits may leave something behind that tastes bad. After frost, the bugs don't seem to come around to bother them.

> **In a nutshell:**
>
> Brick-colored caps; stem covered with fine fibers; growing in clusters, appearing as late as November; purple brown spores.

Remember to take your camera along with your baskets on your autumn hikes. Frequently, you will come upon brick top scenes beautiful enough for a calendar picture.

Cap: 1" to 3" across; dark brick red, often paler or yellowish near the edge; nicely domed and rounded, flatter in age.

Gills: Reach the stem and contact it, but are not attached to it; slightly rounded at the stem; at first yellowish white, becoming greenish and finally purplish brown from the colored spores.

Spore print: Purplish brown.

Stem: Usually hollow when old; slender; covered with fine fibers.

Growth habit: Grows on or around old hardwood stumps and logs. August to November.

Edibility: Good if you find it before the bugs get to it, which may make it taste bitter.

Copycats: The poisonous sulphur tuft (*Naematoloma fasciculare*) is a smaller mushroom with a greenish yellow to orange-yellow cap, olive-tinted young gills attached to the stem, and a bitter taste raw or cooked. The edible and delicious orange stump mushroom (*N. capnoides*) has an orange to yellow-brown cap and gray gills that become colored purplish gray as the spores mature. Like the brick top, both of these species have a purple-brown spore print.

Tip: Brick tops like to grow on the exposed roots of trees blown over by wind. You can spot these trees a long distance away from your car window. So watch for them as you drive, hike, and bicycle in the wild places in the fall.

Gilled; white spores

93 Blewit

Clitocybe nuda (Fries) Bigelow and Smith
(cly-TOSS-sye-bee NEW-dah)

Lepista nuda, Rhodopaxillus nudus, and *Tricholoma personatum* are other names you will find in various guidebooks.

Can you guess why mushroomers commonly call this species "blewit"? Read the description below, listen to the sound of the name, and think about it. (The answer appears on the next page.*)

This species has a lot to offer a mushroomer looking for something special to take home for dinner. For one thing, the large size and lavender-blue color make for easy identification. It often grows in large quantities, too, and has a taste and texture that is widely appreciated. This is another one of the world's really good eating mushrooms, recognized everywhere as a gourmet delicacy.

Blewits prefer to grow through the late fall and early winter in this region. You will rarely find the species in spring and summer. Look for it in leaf dumps and wood debris piles, but keep an eye on lawns, backyards, and golf courses as well. Even with their large size, big clusters, and bright colors, blewits can escape your notice because they can appear in dry, cold weather—at a time you might not expect mushrooms to grow.

You can tell from the number of alternative scientific names I've listed for this species that mycologists have enjoyed shuffling its name around over the years. The name your mushroom guide uses depends upon when the book was published.

In a nutshell: This mushroom is easy to identify because of its late season of growth in lawns and debris, whitish spores, violet bulky cap and stem, and violet fuzz at the swollen base of the stem.

Cap: 2" to about 5" wide; thick and bulky; lilac or violet tinted, sometimes with a brownish color in the center of the cap; edge of the cap often wavy in old age.

Gills: Rounded at the stem and usually not attached to stem; colored like the cap, but fading to dull tones with age.

Spore print: Dull white or pinkish white.

Stem: About 1" to 3" long; short and stout; colored like the cap, often with violet fuzz at the base; base of stem often swollen like a bulb.

Growth habit: Grows in groups in all kinds of debris: leaf and wood chip piles, decomposing organic matter in open places and thin woods; seems to prefer oak leaf dumps in this region. It often grows in rows and arcs in lawns, however. Late August through December.

Edibility: Excellent.

Copycats: Be sure to take a spore print of any purple mushroom as you are learning to identify this species. Remember that blewits have thick stems and a dull white or pinkish white spore print color. If you get a brown or rusty brown print, you likely have a species of *Inocybe* or *Cortinarius* that may be poisonous. Purple-tinted mushrooms that give a heavy pink spore print and have thinner stems are most likely *Entoloma* species (and probably poisonous). Smaller purple mushrooms with skinny stems and bright white spore prints are probably *Mycena* or *Laccaria* species.

Tip: Be sure to recheck the place where you gathered this mushroom, because new crops often appear a few times in succession. Sometimes, if the conditions are right, you can return to the same place over a period of weeks and collect lots of mushrooms.

* And on the name: "blewit" is a corruption of "blue hat."

---

94 Velvet stem mushroom, velvet foot
Flammulina velutipes (Fries) Karsten
(flam-you-LEE-nah vel-you-TIE-pes)

Called *Collybia velutipes* in older guidebooks.

Unlike most of us, the velvet stem mushroom loves winter temperatures. It just doesn't make much of a showing through the warmer months, when most wild mushrooms—and we—come out. Its dark woolly stem covering seems appropriate dress, even though it offers little or no protection in cold weather. Look for it from October through April in rainy weather on dead hardwood stumps and logs, mainly elm. Low, damp areas are a favorite location, so check stumps along streams.

Stem details are important in identifying this species. When young, the stems are smooth, but as they get older, they develop a dark brown velvety covering that starts from the base of the stem and gradually moves upward toward the cap. Combine this feature with the unusual time of growth—the coldest months—and you've got two good aids to help you identify it. This is a very easy mushroom to learn.

This was one of the first mushrooms I learned to identify and eat. It took some time to get used to its firm texture and slimy feel, but now I enjoy it. Anyway, you can't be too picky when it may be the only wild mushroom you can find when you go winter hunting.

In a nutshell:

Small orangish mushrooms preferring cold weather; caps that are slimy when moist; older stems covered with a dark velvet skin; white spore print. Grows in clusters from a common base on elm or other hardwood.

Cap: 1" to 2 ¼" wide; color some shade of reddish brown, orange-brown or yellow- brown; surface slimy in damp weather.

Gills: White to pale yellow; not attached to the stem.

Spore print: White.

Stem: 1" to 4" long, up to ¼" thick; tough texture; when young, smooth with pale yellow to orange-brown color. With age, it develops a dark brown to blackish velvety covering.

Growth habit: Dense clusters, often from a single base on elm or other hardwood. October through April.

Edibility: Good.

Copycats: The deadly galerina, *Galerina autumnalis,* is a very common, deadly poisonous mushroom species that vaguely resembles the velvet stem mushroom. Fortunately, it's easy to separate the two. Among other things, the deadly galerina has a *delicate ring on a non-velvety stem* and *rusty brown spores*. The velvet stem has *no ring on a velvety stem* and *white spores*. Both species may appear at the same time in cold fall weather, into November, so taking a spore print is a must when you are learning to identify velvet stems. If you get a white spore print, you know you don't have the deadly galerina.

Tip: Velvet stems often hide close to the ground. Examine the base of stumps and turn over logs to see if any mushrooms grow on the underside. Growers cultivate this species for market on oak sawdust because the mushroom grows on it so well. Check out the sawdust and debris piles around sawmills.

---

95 ## Green oyster mushroom, late oyster mushroom
Panellus serotinus Fries Kühner
(pa-NELL-lus se-roe-TINE-nus)

Dr. Seuss's Sam doesn't like green eggs and ham, but you may welcome a dish of green oyster mushrooms prepared in your favorite way. They usually taste pleasant after cooking. At other times, they can be too bitter to enjoy. We can't be too particular, though, because mushroom pickings become very slim in this part of the country in November—just the time that green oysters prefer to grow. Cook them slowly for a long time for the best flavor.

"Green oyster" is not a completely accurate name, because the caps can display a rainbow range of color, including shades of gray. Yet they often show some hue of green. From the way they grow in overlapping shelflike clusters on logs and stumps, they resemble the true oyster mushroom, *Pleurotus ostreatus*. Beyond that, the similarities drop off.

In a nutshell:

Greenish yellow, sticky, shell-shaped caps. Grows on dead wood in late fall and early winter.

Like the pattern of the stars in the sky or the migration of the birds, the appearance of this mushroom in late fall and early winter marks the end of the season for most mushroomers. It tells us that the time has come to retire the pocketknife and mushroom basket until next spring, when the morels appear and another season of mushroom madness begins.

Cap: 1" to 4" across; shaped like a clam or oyster shell; dull green or yellowish green, sometimes with brown, gray, or purple tones; sticky surface.

Gills: Pale orange to orangish yellow; run down the stem.

Spore print: Yellowish.

Stem: Short and stubby; hairy; yellowish or brownish.

Edibility: Edible, but sometimes bitter.

Growth habit: Scattered or in groups of shelflike structures, on all kinds of dead wood.

Copycats: The appearance and season of this species make it difficult to confuse with any other. The true oyster mushroom, *Pleurotus ostreatus,* can grow at just about any time of the year if the weather is right, but it has white gills, white spores, and a non-hairy stem.

Tip: This mushroom seems to prefer to grow in deep, dark, damp woods. Unlike most mushrooms, it can grow on almost any kind of dead wood. It's one of the few mushrooms that can grow on cherry wood.

---

96 **Astringent panus**

Panellus stypticus (Bulliard : Fries) Karsten
(pa-NELL-lus STIP-tih-cuss)

Called *Panus stypticus* in older books.

This small and inconspicuous species is one of the most fascinating and beautiful mushrooms of the woods. You can find it practically year-round, except in the coldest winter months.

It has the amazing ability to glow in the dark. The greenish phosphorescence comes from the same chemical reactions seen in fireflies. Although fireflies and mushrooms are biologically unrelated, when nature finds a good thing—like biochemical light—it likes to spread it among various life forms. For fireflies, the light helps them find mates. Certain sea creatures use the same light to attract food. No one knows why a mushroom needs to glow in the dark except, perhaps, to enchant the forest at night.

When I was walking through the woods one night, I found this mushroom growing in vertical rows on an old rotting tree stump. In the darkness, the scene looked like a miniature skyscraper at night with some of the windows lit. Another time, while I was walking along a country road in the dark, I found it growing on the top of a low stump in a beautiful, luminous circular cluster the size and shape of a rose. A sight like that takes a mushroomer's breath away.

In a nutshell: This is the only white-spored, gilled mushroom species in the woods in this region that looks like little clamshells, grows in clusters or rows on dead hardwood, and glows in the dark.

Cap: Small, ¼" to ½" in size; whitish tan color; tough, slightly scaly, and clamshell shaped.

Gills: Close together, colored much like the cap. Under a magnifying glass, you can see thin veins connecting the gills under the cap.

Spore print: White.

Stem: Short; comes from the side of the cap; colored like the cap, but darker near the base.

Growth habit: In rows or clusters on stumps and logs of deciduous trees in the woods. June to December.

Edibility: Inedible. Tough and bitter; may be somewhat poisonous.

Copycats: It resembles species of *Crepidotus* and *Paxillus,* but these have yellowish to brown spore prints, not white. They do not glow in the dark.

Tip: Bring some of these mushrooms home and put them in your bedroom. You can watch their soft green glow as you fall asleep.

---

97 **Oyster mushroom, woods oyster, tree oyster**
Pleurotus ostreatus (Jaquin : Fries) Kummer complex
(plur-OH-tus owe-stree-AY-tus)

Known locally as oysters.

You can find oysters in the central Pennsylvania woods, but they are not the kind you find at the seashore. These mushrooms look remarkably like oyster shells and, in some imaginative people's opinion, even taste like oysters. Everyone should get to know this species because it's easy to learn, easy to find, and is regarded as one of the world's best edible mushrooms.

If you've used the stale, dried-out oyster mushrooms grown for the supermarkets, you are in for a treat when you try them gathered fresh from the woods. Sometimes, a real bumper crop appears on a stump or log. The trick is to beat the bugs, because they like oyster mushrooms as much as we do.

Oyster mushrooms generally appear when a few warm, humid days follow a day or two of cold rainy weather. Although these conditions can happen at any time of the year in this region, the fall and spring months usually offer the best times for oystering. You can also find this mushroom in the winter, though, during periods of warmer temperatures. Watch for them, especially through the annual early "January thaw" that happens here.

Mushroom scientists consider this mushroom to be "complex"—comprising a group of closely related and very similar-looking species that have not been defined yet. At this time, no one knows how many separate species authorities will finally find in the oyster mushroom. It really doesn't matter to those of us who appreciate its edible qualities and are not interested in splitting hairs.

> **In a nutshell:**
>
> White or tan to gray shelflike clusters on hardwood; smooth, tender, oyster shell–shaped caps; white gills; white spores.

Cap: 2" to 8" across; white, but sometimes gray, tan, or brown; fan or oyster shaped; smooth, moist, and tender; often has a sweet odor and a mild taste, raw or cooked.

Gills: White; run down the stem.

Spore print: White or pale lavender.

Stem: Off to the side (lateral), but often there is not much of a stem.

Growth habit: Grows year-round in shelflike forms or overlapping rows on hardwood stumps and logs. Prefers aspen in this region.

Edibility: Very good.

Copycats: Angel wings (*Pleurocybella porrigens,* also called *Pleurotus porrigens*) is a smaller, thinner white species that grows on conifers. It is edible, and while most people like it better than *Pleurotus ostreatus,* some think it's inferior. Edible *Pleurotus populinus* is very similar to

P. ostreatus but has a pale whitish tan spore print. Species of *Panus, Panellus, Schizophyllum,* and *Lentinus* more or less resemble the oyster mushroom but, for one thing, they are distinctly more tough textured. *Lentinus* species have notable saw-toothed gill edges. None of these look-alikes are dangerous, but avoid any shelf mushrooms that do not smell good.

Tip: Try growing your own backyard oyster mushroom garden by this very old method. The next time you have some extra oyster mushrooms, find a freshly cut hardwood log or stump and lay the mushrooms, gill side down, on the cut sections of the wood. To keep them from drying out for as long as possible, set a flat rock on top of the mushrooms. Spores will fall from the gills and, if you are lucky, some of the spores will germinate and grow into the wood. After the mushroom mycelium is established, you could get mushroom crops for several years with two or three harvests a year if the conditions are right. Be patient. It may take a few weeks or months for mushrooms to appear.

If you try this method in your backyard, you can improve your chances of success by watering the wood a couple of times a week for a month. Don't use hard water; the dissolved minerals can inhibit the growth of the mushrooms. Use rainwater or distilled water instead.

---

98 Bell-shaped fuzzy foot
Xeromphalina campanella (Bataille : Fries) Kühner and Maire
(zer-om-fa-LINE-nah cam-pa-NELL-lah)

You will find this species named *Omphalia campanella* and *Omphalopsis campanella* in some other books.

If you have avoided couch potato syndrome and enjoy walking in the hemlock forests of this region from spring into early winter, you certainly have seen this pretty, miniature mushroom. It grows so prolifically that hundreds of specimens bristle from hemlock and other rotting conifer logs and stumps. Few other mushrooms grow in such huge numbers.

Because each individual mushroom is tiny, you must use a magnifying glass to appreciate its delicate beauty. The orange-yellow caps of fuzzy foot mushrooms are bell shaped, with a pit or depression in the center. Fine lines radiate from the center of the cap to the edge. The brown stem can be thinner than a toothpick.

Most mushroom authorities consider this mushroom inedible—or too small to bother with. At least two old-time authors call it a decent table mushroom, though. I know mushroomers who eat the bell-shaped fuzzy foot frequently. Sometimes it may be the only edible species available when you are hunting mushrooms for dinner. Due to its small size, collecting this mushroom can be tedious. It is easier to harvest with scissors than with a knife.

In a nutshell: Tiny, yellow-rusty mushrooms; with a deep depression or pit in the center of the cap; with a very skinny dark brown stem that has brown fuzz at the base; not bitter-tasting when raw. Grows by the hundreds on old coniferous wood.

Cap: ¼" to 1" across; thin, tough, and depressed in the center of the cap; delicate lines on the surface from the center to the edge of the cap; yellow-rusty to dull yellow color; tastes mild raw.

Gills: Yellow; running down the stem; connected by veins on the underside of the cap (use a magnifying glass).

Spore print: White.

Stem: ½" to 1 ½" long; very thin; pale brown; hollow; with brown hairs at the base.

Growth habit: In large numbers on dead coniferous logs and stumps. May to November.

Edibility: Edible.

Copycats: Certain other *Xeromphalina* species grow on hardwoods, but not conifers. Some taste bitter raw. Some have longer stems than the bell-shaped fuzzy foot. *Mycena* species lack the deep pit in the center of the cap. The deadly autumn galerina *(Galerina autumnalis)* is typically larger and has *brown* spores, so be sure to take a spore print.

Tip: When you go hiking with your camera, take a close-up or macro lens with you so that you can photograph this beautiful, tiny species when you find it. The magnified images are impressive when mounted in small frames.

Neither gilled nor pored

99 Winter chanterelle, funnel chanterelle

Cantharellus infundibuliformis Fries, *sensu* Smith and Moore
(can-tha-RELL-lus in-fun-dih-byu-lih-FOR-miss)

This is another species of the world-famous *Cantharellus* genus of mushrooms. While it may not stir as much passion as certain other chanterelles, some mushroomers consider it a special delicacy anyway. Part of its appeal comes from its habit of growing into the winter, when wild mushrooms are very scarce. If you are interested in winter mushrooming, this is certainly one worth knowing about, even if you dread the thought of learning to pronounce—and remember—its scientific name.

Don't let that tongue twister put you off. *Cantharellus* means "a small goblet or wine cup," and *infundibuliformis* innocently translates as "funnel-form." So the scientific name simply means "a small wine cup in the shape of a funnel," which describes its appearance very well. If you prefer to call it funnel chanterelle, other knowledgeable mushroomers will know what you are talking about. But think of how you'll impress your family and friends if you can casually toss the scientific name around. That, alone, could be your incentive to learn to pronounce it.

You can find this species from July into early December, so it's an appropriate addition to the collection of winter mushrooms in this book. At times, this may be the only early winter mushroom you will find on your outings. It seems to tolerate drier weather than most mushrooms.

Not many mushroomers pick this species. Maybe they feel that it's too small to bother with or that there are too many similar-looking small hollow-stemmed chanterelles to deal with. Their neglect is our advantage.

In a nutshell: Dark brown smooth cap; lemon yellow hollow stem; yellow-cream or white spores.

Cap: 1" to 2" across; becoming funnel shaped with age; smooth; dark yellow-brown to dark brown color; wavy edge.

Gills: Thick, forked and branched; running down the stem; yellowish, becoming grayish or brownish.

Spore print: Yellowish to cream color.

Stem: 1" to 4" long; thin, smooth, and hollow; yellowish or lemon yellow.

Growth habit: Cool, damp, shaded evergreen forests; in groups or clusters in sphagnum moss in wet places, mossy ground, and on rotting coniferous wood. July to December.

Edibility: Good.

Copycats: *Cantharellus minor,* the small chanterelle, is smaller than the winter and completely yellow. The trumpet chanterelle, *C. tubaeformis,* makes a white spore print. Both are edible. *C. ignicolor,* the flame chanterelle, has a yellow-orange cap and brownish gills. There are others. Check your identification books for further details on the species listed here and others.

Tip: Look for this mushroom in cool, woodsy, mossy places. It likes to grow along the banks and edges of dams, lakes, streams, swamps, and bogs. Sometimes you can't find it anywhere else.

Pored (polypores)

100 Turkey tail

Trametes versicolor (Linnaeus : Fries) Pilát
(tra-MEE-tees VER-sih-co-lor)

Listed as *Coriolus versicolor, Polystictus versicolor,* and *Polyporus versicolor* in certain other guidebooks.

Mushrooms never stop entertaining us. Even people with weak powers of imagination can't help noticing the resemblance of this beautiful mushroom to a tiny turkey's fanned-out tail. Each little cap displays a spectacular array of concentric color bands in hues of white, grays, dull yellows, blues, reds, browns, and black (and even greens from algae growth). Just about anywhere in the country, at any time of the year, you may see this wood-loving polypore growing in multi-tiered clusters in the forest. Although the mushroom looks delicate and fragile, the texture is quite tough and leathery. Surprisingly durable, it can survive and continue growing after severe droughts and winter temperatures, sometimes for a number of years. Dead hardwoods are its favorite food. But this innocent-looking little fungus can also be a wolf-in-turkey's-clothing parasite, destroying the heartwood of fruit trees and others.

For thousands of years, Asian herbalists have used turkey tail mushrooms in their healing work. In China it has been called *yun zhi*; in Japan, *karawatake*. It was one of the first fungi to provide a modern drug for treating cancer. Mushroomers in the know use the tough caps as a pleasant mushroom-flavored chewing gum while walking in the woods. They also boil them to make a healthful tea or broth for soup.

> **In a nutshell:**
>
> Small, leathery, stemless shelflike mushrooms with rainbow-colored bands. Grows in overlapping tiers on hardwood.

Cap: 1" to 4" across; fan shaped; with bands of color that almost span the rainbow; alternating smooth and velvety zones; thin, tough, and leathery.

Pores: White.

Spore print: White.

Stem: None, or very short, at the edge of the cap.

Growth habit: Dense overlapping clusters on hardwood. May to December, but may survive for years.

Edibility: Edible and healthful, but too tough to eat.

Copycats: The hairy turkey tail, *Coriolus hirsutis,* is slightly thicker, hairy, and has only grayish and yellowish to brownish color bands. The false turkey tail, *Stereum ostrea,* does not show distinct pores under the cap through a magnifying glass. *Hirschioporus pergamenus,* the violet-pored turkey tail, grows on conifer wood, is less dramatically colored than turkey tail, and has violet-tinted pores. All of these are probably edible, though tough, and may have healthful properties like the turkey tail.

Tip: Turkey tails dry easily and are great to use in craft-work, such as jewelry making.

winter mushrooms

90   Common inky cap, *Coprinus atramentarius,* p. 190

91   Scaly pholiota, *Pholiota squarrosa,* p. 191

92   Brick top, *Hypholoma sublateritium*, p. 193

93   Blewit, *Clitocybe nuda*, p. 195

94   Velvet stem mushroom, *Flammulina velutipes*, p. 196

95 Green oyster mushroom, *Panellus serotinus,* p. 198

96 Astringent panus, *Panellus stypticus,* p. 199

97 Oyster mushroom, *Pleurotus ostreatus,* p. 200

98 Bell-shaped fuzzy foot, *Xeromphalina campanella,* p. 202

99 Winter chanterelle, *Cantharellus infundibuliformis,* p. 204

100   Turkey tail, *Trametes versicolor,* p. 205

When human beings appeared on the earth, one of the first questions on everyone's mind was, "Where can I find something to eat?" Obviously, we are here, so it must not have taken long to discover that the woods were full of food. The invention of agriculture eventually freed us from our potluck dependence on wild places for our meals. Yet people all over the world continue to gather wild food. In some countries it's still a primary way of life. Even in the most modern places—such as the United States, with our lives surrounded by computers, television, fast cars, and sophisticated agricultural technology—people continue to use foods that they gather from natural places, mainly for health, fun, and recreation. I have friends who make good wine from wild elderberries, tangy cider from wild apples, healthful salads with wild dandelion greens, delicious cookies with wild walnuts, and exceptional dishes from wild fish and game. But I don't know many people in this country who gather wild mushrooms, although they are one of the most sought-after wild foods in many other countries.

Mushrooms are a healthful food. Humans can't digest much of their high protein content, yet they are a good source of vitamins, minerals, and enzymes. And with their beautiful colors, distinctive texture, and delicious, unique flavors, they can add interest and zest to the diet. They can serve as the main part of a recipe or be used as accessories to enhance a wide variety of dishes, sparking up the menu. When you learn to gather your own edible wild mushrooms and bring them home to prepare immediately, you have food as fresh as it is possible to find anywhere. This is an important consideration, because fresh food loses certain vitamins, enzymes, flavors, and other nutritional value when it is stored.

We don't trust mushrooms here in the United States because most of us are unfamiliar with them. We tend to think of them as especially dangerous. While it's true that there are a few very bad mushroom "characters" out there, the dangers of learning to pick and use wild mushrooms are overrated. (The hazards from eating the wrong mushroom, however, are not.) Wild mushrooms aren't the only things growing outdoors that can harm you. Many people don't realize that they can get just as sick from eating the wrong wild green plant's leaves, berries, roots, seeds, and so on as from eating the wrong mushroom. Some common wild and garden plants, such as poison ivy, poison hemlock root, flowering dogwood tree berries, and privet hedge berries (to mention just a few), can be deadly poisonous. We don't hesitate to eat such delicacies as wild strawberries when we find them because we are more familiar with green plants than with fungi. Fortunately, of the thousands of mushroom species that grow in our area, only about half a dozen in any season are deadly poisonous. With a little determination, anyone can learn to identify a variety of safe, delicious mushrooms and steer clear of those few perilous mushroom personalities that deserve a wide berth.

While poisonous mushrooms have no universal earmarks, certain *Amanita* species that are easy to avoid are responsible for most of the serious mushroom poisonings here and around the world. Perhaps their appeal comes from their attractive, appetizing appearance and, to untrained eyes, their close resemblance to certain edible mushrooms. Survivors tell us that they even taste good. Clearly, then, the first thing a beginning mushroomer must know is to be able to identify amanitas with absolute certainty—and then avoid them. All *Amanita* species have white spores; white gills that are unattached to the stem; a ring on the stem; and a sack, swelling, sheath, or scaly bulb at the base of the stem. Some *Amanita* species are edible, but don't eat any mushroom that has these features, unless you are a real amanita expert!

One of the most widespread and deadly *Amanita* species is the notorious and all-too-common destroying angel, or, as it's called in this region, angel of death. The "angel" is actually a group of several look-alike species such as *Amanita verna, A. virosa, A. bisporigera,* and white forms of *A. phalloides.* All of these species can display a striking pure white color that some people call "ghostly white." Merely handling these toxic amanitas can't poison you, but it's safest to leave them out of your collecting basket.

While you may feel that no one could possibly make a mistake and eat a poisonous mushroom that you

Structure of an *Amanita* mushroom

bring home to study, consider the curiosity of your pets—and your friends. There are reports of cats being attracted to dry specimens of the fly mushroom, *Amanita muscaria.* Although this poisonous species usually isn't deadly poisonous to humans who eat it, it has killed cats. This species also sickened a local resident several years ago. A knowledgeable mushroomer, while taking a walk on his lunch break, found several handsome fly mushroom specimens and brought them back to decorate his desk at work, never intending that anyone would eat them. At the end of the day, after he had gone home, a fellow employee found them, thought they were edible, and ate them (after all, an "expert" had gathered them). He recovered, but only after a few days of severe stomach and intestinal distress.

This region hosts a few other deadly mushrooms besides amanitas. Unlike *Amanita* species, though, many of these have no general earmarks. To avoid getting into trouble with these, heed the old saying, "Don't eat any mushroom that you are not absolutely sure of." I would add another important piece of advice: if you want to learn to pick edible wild mushrooms for food, you should not use this book as your sole guide. Remember that learning wild mushrooms is a *study*. Usually, people who collect wild mushrooms for food have been taught by someone who knows edible species with certainty, or they have devoted much time to studying the mushrooms' physical details and historical reputation from as many books as they can find. Ideally, they have done both. For anyone interested in learning to eat wild mushrooms, there is yet another valuable old saying, this one from China: "Make haste slowly." In other words, don't be in a hurry to expand the list of mushrooms that you are learning to eat. Adding two or three new species to your list of edibles in a year is a good pace. As an eager beginner, ready to go out and conquer the world of fungi, this may seem like slow progress to you. Consider, though, that most people in this country can't pick even *one* edible wild mushroom in a whole lifetime.

Some further precautions to keep in mind:

- Practically any food, including any edible mushroom species, can cause problems for someone who is sensitive to it. While these sensitivities usually do not lead to life-threatening situations, they can be quite uncomfortable. From experience, we learn about the foods that we need to avoid early in life. Remember that each new species of edible mushroom is a new food to your body. Smart mushroomers test their sensitivity to a new mushroom by sampling only a small amount the first time they eat it. If they get unpleasant reactions, they know to avoid eating that particular species again.

- Don't eat any mushroom raw unless you know for certain that it is good to eat uncooked. Some of our best and most popular wild mushrooms, such as morels, honey mushrooms, and chanterelles, don't sit well on the stomach if eaten raw. Heat breaks down their indigestible or somewhat toxic properties.

- Eat only fresh mushrooms. Consisting mainly of protein material, fungi decompose like meat. We all know the potential problems that can come from eating spoiled meat, before or after cooking.

- Don't rely on the old-fashioned "tests" for poisonous mushrooms such as the "silver coin in the pot" test. It's a myth that a coin will turn a dark color from reacting to a mushroom toxin. Many people have become ill from relying on this method of detecting poisonous mushrooms. And feeding mushrooms to an animal and watching its reaction is not a valid test, because animals can process food differently from humans. There is no simple test for poisonous mushrooms.

- Overindulging is a common cause of discomfort from eating mushrooms. They may be delicious to eat, but fungi are rich and contain some proteins that we may not digest easily. So the next time you gather a big basket of edible mushrooms, think moderation!

- Small children in the crawling stage are particularly vulnerable to mushroom poisoning—or poisoning from any plant. The problem is that these youngsters tend to taste or eat anything they can find. Mushroom species that may be only moderately poisonous to an adult can cause much more severe reactions in a small child and can even cause death, mainly because of the difference in body size. It may be a good idea to remove toxic mushrooms and poisonous green plants that are growing in the lawn and elsewhere around your home if there are small children of grazing age nearby.

Mushroom Poisons

Poisonous mushrooms contain several different kinds of toxins. To simplify the discussion, I divide the toxins below into four groups: deadly toxins, gastrointestinal toxins, mind-altering toxins, and sweat-producing toxins.

Deadly Toxins

Eating toxic species of the *Amanita* genus causes the most mushroom deaths. It's easy to know if you have *Amanita* mushroom species, because they are clearly earmarked. A few other species, just as deadly, are scattered through other genera and don't look like amanitas. Obviously, it's important to avoid mistaking these for edible mushrooms. The deadly poisonous *Conocybe filaris* and *Galerina autumnalis* resemble certain hallucinogenic species, such as *Psilocybe semilanceata* and *P. caerulipes.* To inexperienced collectors, these can be a real threat. Yet it's easy to tell the difference with a spore print, because *Psilocybe* species have black spores, and *Conocybe* and *Galerina* species have some shade of brown spores. Deadly *Lepiota castanea* and *L. josserandii* have some features of the edible parasol mushroom *(Macrolepiota procera),* but unlike it, their stems are scaly and have no ring. Finally, *Cortinarius gentilis* must not be confused with edible species in the same genus. Its deadly threat leads some authors to recommend not eating any *Cortinarius* mushroom species. A good homework assignment for beginning mushroomers is to study all of these dangerous species carefully in as many guidebooks as they can find. If you are short on books, a trip to your local college or university library would be worthwhile.

If you suspect that someone has eaten deadly poisonous mushrooms, immediately induce vomiting and then rush him or her to the hospital. (If the mushrooms were eaten more than three or four hours earlier, they may have passed from the stomach. Vomiting may be of little value in this case.) An old-time mushroomer's way to induce vomiting that still works well is to take a spoonful of mustard seed powder stirred in a cup of warm water, followed by several more cups of warm water. Then wait a few seconds and tickle the back of the throat with the fingers. Continue the treatment until the vomited fluids look clear.

Gastrointestinal Toxins

This class represents the most common kind of mushroom poisoning. Symptoms can begin shortly after eating the mushrooms and may continue for several hours. Abdominal cramps, diarrhea, nausea, and vomiting are typical. Depending on the poisonous species, symptoms may range from mild to severe. Usually hospital attention isn't required (unless the symptoms themselves merit it). Yet a visit to the hospital can ease the mind of someone who has eaten a toxic mushroom, such as the jack o' lantern *(Omphalotus olearius)*, in the following category.

Mind-Altering Toxins

Many people are mainly interested in learning about wild mushrooms so that they can find "magic mushrooms." There are good reasons not to eat them or even collect them, however.

Several hallucinogenic species of *Psilocybe* and *Panaeolus* that contain psilocybin and related psychoactive substances grow in this region. *It is illegal to use, possess, or even gather these species for study.* Possessing even one specimen can be a felony. Merely picking a specimen and holding it in your hand can be considered possession. In some places in the United States, police will secretly keep an eye on a patch of illegal mushrooms and arrest the first person who picks them. Several years ago, a mushroomer was arrested after showing some "friends" a dried hallucinogenic mushroom specimen he saved as a curiosity. Don't let that happen to you!

It's both amusing and frightening to realize that you can commit a federal crime simply by taking home a basket of mushrooms to study. In some states, authorities consider any mushroom picker a potential magic mushroom hunter. While officials may not be able to identify mushrooms by sight, they do have laboratory chemical tests that indicate the presence of illegal psychoactive substances. So if you think that the magic mushroom species you have found is too obscure to be identified by the authorities, remember that the chemical test is available in all states.

Many mushroomers will argue that I should not include psychoactive species of *Panaeolus* and *Psilocybe* in the poisonous mushroom section of this book. Aside from some possible slight, brief nausea, these mushrooms really don't make us sick in the traditional way. Their typical effects are mental ones: distortion of perceptions, altered states of awareness with deep spiritual insights, and wild hallucinations. These mind-bending experiences usually last a few hours. If someone unfamiliar with magic mushrooms unknowingly eats one, the experience can be frightening and traumatic, often involving a trip to the emergency room. Once the patient feels assured that he or she is not dying or going insane, the person usually calms down until the effects pass.

Other hallucinogenic mushroom species growing in this region are legal to possess, because they do not contain psilocybin or other illegal substances. While these species may be quite common, their use is definitely not recommended.

One of the most common of the legal hallucinogenic mushrooms is the fly mushroom, *Amanita muscaria.* It is definitely poisonous, but its varieties apparently contain different proportions of the poisonous and hallucinogenic biochemical agents. In some places, the poisonous agents in the local fly mushroom are low enough and the hallucinogenic agents high enough that it can be eaten reasonably safely and with powerful psychedelic effects. For example, people of Siberia have used it for thousands of years in religious and shamanic rituals. To reduce the poisonous effects, they dry the mushroom before eating it. The varieties of this species in our region, however, seem to have high levels of toxin and low levels of hallucinogenic agents. If you eat fly mushrooms from this part of the country, you will probably become very sick and not have any noticeable psychedelic experiences. The "trip" you take will most likely be to the hospital. I know of a few local people who have tried using the fly mushroom like the Siberians—but not one would repeat the experience.

The genus *Gymnopilus* has some interesting mind-altering species. Most famous is *Gymnopilus spectabilis,* the big laughing gym mushroom. As the name suggests, it makes a person laugh after eating it, sometimes for hours. Even the most mundane activities, such as tying your shoes or looking at your face in a mirror, can be outrageously funny. Even worrying that you might die from uncontrolled laughter can bring on more hilarious laughter. The active biochemical principle in this genus is unidentified, so these mushrooms are legal to possess.

If you are getting ready to head for the woods to hunt for big laughing gym mushrooms, though, think again. It's been reported that *G. spectabilis* occasionally contains psilocybin or related compounds. If the gyms you find test positive for these chemicals, you are breaking the law by merely possessing them. Besides, this species sometimes contains monomethylhydrazine, which you may recognize as rocket fuel. This is a very poisonous substance with unpredictable and quirky properties. When a person eats mushrooms that contain it, sometimes it has no effect; at other times, it kills. The same toxin appears in the false morel, *Gyromitra esculenta,* and has caused deaths. So considering the legal and health-related risks of laughing gyms, it's smart to avoid them altogether.

Sweat-Producing Toxins

Of the various kinds of poisonous mushrooms, some of the strangest are those that promote heavy perspiration. *Clitocybe dealbata* falls into this odd category. Its ingestion may cause diarrhea and salivation, but it mainly triggers profuse perspiration that can last for hours. Species that contain this kind of toxin are common in this region. They are usually not fatally poisonous to adults, but they can cause worry and great discomfort for the person who eats them.

Final Thoughts on Mushroom Toxins

While four of the main classes of mushroom poisons are listed above, others can cause mild to serious effects. Again, if you want to eat mushrooms, the best way to avoid mushroom poisoning is never to eat any species that you cannot identify with certainty.

After all this talk about mushroom poisoning, you may wonder why anyone in his or her right mind would consider learning to eat wild mushrooms. But remember that people all over the world, including in this country, safely gather wild mushrooms and eat them all the time. The news media love to report deaths from mushroom poisonings, but how often do we hear those sensational stories? Fatalities from eating deadly poisonous mushrooms are rare.

Who gets poisoned? People from other countries who mistake toxic mushrooms that grow here for edible mushrooms that they gather back home. People who use simple field or home "tests," like the silver coin in the pot. People who use "intuition" to separate poisonous and edible mushrooms. People who don't test their mushroom sensitivities. People who take chances by eating mushrooms they are unsure of, and people who eat mushrooms that grow in chemically poisoned places.

Don't be any of these people, and you can learn to pick and eat wild mushrooms.

Mushrooms in the Kitchen

After you get your edible mushrooms home, you have to get them ready for cooking or preserving. They will probably need cleaning, but if you have done some preliminary work before you put them in your collecting basket, your job will be much easier in the kitchen. At this point, beginning mushroomers often dump their collection of edibles in a pan of water for fast cleaning. Gilled mushrooms treated this way take up and retain a large amount of water in their structure. This may be acceptable if you plan to use your mushrooms in soups, stews, or other dishes with high water content. But if you use these waterlogged mushrooms to make drier dishes, such as sautés, you will have to contend with excess moisture in the pan. Simply wiping the caps and stems with a moist cloth or paper napkin is a better way to clean mushrooms. To remove debris from the undersides, careful brushing will often do the job. Some mushroomers pucker their lips and briskly blow on the gills to dislodge the material.

You can find mushroom recipes everywhere. Many cookbooks have recipes for supermarket mushrooms. You can substitute wild mushrooms in many of these recipes, if you are familiar with the cooking qualities of different species. This awareness comes from experience. To know the cooking potential of a mushroom, many people simply sauté it in butter. By preparing it in this way, you get an idea of the basic flavor and texture to guide you in using the mushroom in more elaborate recipes. Many field guides include suggestions and recipes for cooking individual species.

Instead of eating your mushrooms fresh, you can preserve them for future meals. Most vegetable preserving methods will work well. Freezing is a good choice if you first blanch the mushrooms in hot water. Many people prefer to sauté them first, in butter or oil, before packaging them for the freezer. In times past, mushroomers strung their finds like beads to dry over the kitchen stove. Now you can use electric food dryers that hold loads of sliced mushrooms and dehydrate them quickly.

The flavor of certain edible mushroom species improves from drying. Chemical reactions in the dehydration process intensify flavors and bring out odors that were unnoticeable in the mushrooms' fresh state. Many mushroomers like to dry morels (*Morchella* species) and black trumpets (*Craterellus fallax*) instead of eating them fresh for this reason. I know several chefs who always have jars of these dried mushrooms on their kitchen shelves.

Cooking mushrooms in your kitchen is easy and flexible, but there are other ways to do it. A chef friend carries a little pan, matches, a small bottle of oil, and a packet of herbs and spices when he goes mushrooming in the woods. If he finds edible species, he gathers small pieces of dry wood and builds a fire. While waiting for the fire to build up, he cleans his collection with a paper napkin and a small brush. Then he cooks his mushrooms on the spot. His wild dishes are always delicious and unusual. It's fun to go mushrooming with him. Long ago, I learned that it's good to have friends who like to cook mushrooms.

You can spend a lot of time reading your guidebooks, but you will only be able to identify many species when you get out of the house and study mushrooms growing in their natural environment. Only then will you gain the confidence to collect wild mushrooms and prepare your own mouthwatering dishes.

For examples of some of the ways you can prepare wild mushrooms, I offer this selection of recipes.

Sautéed Chicken Breast with Black Trumpets
(*Craterellus fallax* or *C. cornucopioides*)

by Anne Quinn Corr

4	boneless and skinless chicken breasts (chicken cutlets)
¼	cup flour
	salt and pepper to taste
3	tablespoons clarified butter, divided
2	cups black trumpets
¼	cup white wine
1 ½	cups chicken stock
	several sprigs fresh thyme

1 tablespoon soft butter
minced parsley for garnish

Pound out the cutlets so they will cook evenly. Combine the flour and salt and pepper in a cake pan and dredge each cutlet in the mixture, shaking off the excess. Heat 2 tablespoons of the clarified butter in a pan, and when it is hot, add the chicken cutlets and sauté until nicely browned, about 3–4 minutes on each side. Remove them from the pan and hold in a warm oven while you make the sauce. Add the additional 1 tablespoon of clarified butter to the sauté pan and add the black trumpets, cooking them until they soften a little. Add the wine, the chicken stock, and 2 sprigs of thyme. Cook over a high heat until the liquid reduces by half. Whisk in the softened butter at the end of the cooking time, and season to taste with salt and pepper. Remove the cooked thyme. Top with minced parsley and fresh thyme.

Cream of Hen of the Woods (Grifola frondosa) Soup

by Karen Croyle

4–6 cups *Grifola frondosa* (or other mushroom), cleaned and diced
2 tablespoons butter
32 ounces chicken or beef stock, canned or homemade
1–2 cups cream (depends on your taste—I use 2)
¼ cup *cold* water
¼ cup cornstarch

Sauté the diced mushroom in butter for 20–30 minutes. (*G. frondosa* responds well to long, slow cooking; other mushrooms will not take as long.) In a large pot, combine the stock and cream. Bring to a simmer, stirring occasionally. When the mushroom is done, take ½ to ¾ cup of the cooked mushroom and purée it in a food processor until fine. Add the puréed and diced mushroom to the stock/cream mixture and bring to a boil. Mix together the *cold* water and cornstarch until smooth. Slowly add this to the boiling soup, stirring constantly until thickened. You can add more of the cornstarch and cold water mixture until the soup is the desired thickness. Serve.

Chanterelles in Madeira Sauce*

by John Haag

2	cups fresh chanterelles in ½" dice
2	cups light cream
1	cup dried apricots, minced
5–6	shallots, peeled and minced
½	cup finely chopped fresh parsley
⅛	teaspoon grated nutmeg
2	tablespoons Madeira wine (Marsala or sherry may be substituted)

In a saucepan, combine chanterelles, cream, and apricots. Simmer over very low heat until liquid is reduced to about ¼ of its original volume. Add shallots, parsley, and nutmeg. Continue to simmer, stirring almost constantly, for a few more minutes, until liquid is almost evaporated. Mix in Madeira and serve.

Cook's note: This makes an excellent hors d'oeuvre when served hot on thin slices of baguette or in tiny shells of pastry or phyllo dough.

* This recipe won the Acclamation Award at the 1989 Centre County (Pennsylvania) Chefs' Picnic.

Creamy Sulfur Mushroom (*Laetiporus sulphureus*) Soup

by Corene Johnston

1	quart light cream
2	teaspoons unsalted butter
6–8	shallots, peeled and minced
1	vegetable bouillon cube, preferably unsalted
2	cups tender parts of fresh sulfur mushroom in ¼" dice (be careful not to include any of the tougher portion, close to the mushroom's point of attachment to its host wood)
3–4	tablespoons cream sherry
	salt to taste
	croutons

Pour cream into a fairly wide, shallow pan and simmer on low heat until reduced to ⅔ of its original volume. When cream is almost fully reduced, melt butter in a 1 ½-quart saucepan over low heat. Add shallots and sauté until the shallots become translucent. Leave on low heat. Pour cream into shallots, add bouillon cube, and stir until dissolved. Add mushrooms, stir, cover, and simmer on low for about 10 minutes. Mushrooms should be tender but retain some texture. Add sherry, turn heat up slightly, and stir for about one minute.

Taste. If you've used unsalted bouillon, add salt to taste. If you've used salted bouillon, additional salt will probably not be necessary and may overwhelm the subtle mushroom flavor.

Ladle into bowls, and float a few croutons on each for garnish.

Cook's note: This is a rich and filling soup. For a satisfying supper after a day of foraging, serve it with a very simple salad, topped by a tangy but not domineering dressing (mesclun mix dressed with raspberry vinaigrette is perfect). Add a really crusty bread, suitable for dunking in the soup, and fill glasses with a pinot grigio.

JJ's Buttons: Pasture Mushroom *(Agaricus campestris)* Hors d'Oeuvres

by Judith Jubb

12	partly expanded pasture mushrooms with stems
¼	cup olive oil
¼	cup Worcestershire sauce
½	teaspoon dried oregano or 2 tablespoons fresh basil, finely chopped
2	medium garlic cloves, finely chopped or run through a garlic press
⅛	teaspoon salt—sea salt preferred
½	cup finely grated medium cheddar cheese
½	cup finely grated Monterey Jack or Swiss cheese

Clean the mushrooms and cut off the stems at the cap. Finely chop the stems to make about 1 cup. Stir the olive oil, Worcestershire sauce, oregano or basil, garlic, and salt in a bowl. Add the chopped mushroom stems to the bowl and mix. Slowly add the shredded cheeses into the bowl, shaking and occasionally stirring to mix. Generously fill the mushroom caps with the mix from the bowl. Pack firmly and mound up.

Bake in a toaster oven at 300° for 15–20 minutes, or broil in an oven at low temperature until the cheese is melted and the mushroom caps are thoroughly hot but still firm. Avoid crisping. Serve hot.

Open-Faced Mushroom Ravioli with a Rosemary Cream Sauce

by Chef Jason Kroboth

The Sauce
1   teaspoon olive oil
1   teaspoon shallots
1   ounce white wine
1   cup heavy cream
3   sprigs rosemary
1   chopped garlic clove
    salt and pepper

For Mushrooms
2   ounces butter
1   cup sliced oyster, chanterelle, and black trumpet mushrooms (you may substitute any of your favorite fungi)
    salt and pepper

1   6" x 9" pasta sheet
2   tablespoons diced tomato concasse

For sauce: Sauté shallots in olive oil and deglaze with white wine. Reduce by half. Add cream and reduce by about ¼, and then add the fresh rosemary. Keep reducing until thick.

For mushrooms: Sauté mushrooms in butter and then add garlic. Season with salt and pepper to taste.

Boil pasta in salted water until *al dente*.

For assembly: Cut pasta into four equal parts and place in a pool of the rosemary cream sauce. Top with mushrooms and garnish with tomatoes.

Finally, I proudly offer this versatile gem for mycophagists (mushroom eaters).

Bill Russell's Super Simple Mushroom Recipe for Any Edible Species

edible mushrooms
butter
popcorn seasoning

Sauté mushrooms in butter. Sprinkle with popcorn seasoning. Serve warm.

In supermarkets, gourmet food shops, and health food stores, you will find a bewildering array of popcorn seasonings. Each one will give your sautéed mushrooms a special flavor.

Mushrooms can grow in enormous quantities. In a good season, you can practically fill the bed of a small truck with honey mushrooms if you take the time to collect them. When you find such a large quantity of mushrooms on your collecting trips, it's good to remember the way of the Native Americans: take only what you can use and share. Leave the rest to Nature—or to the next collector who comes along.

References

The following authoritative sources offer guidelines for edibility as well as detailed information about the mushrooms described in this book.

Arora, David. *Mushrooms Demystified*. Berkeley, Calif.: Ten Speed Press, 1979.

Barron, George. *Mushrooms of Northeast North America*. Renton, Wash.: Lone Pine Publishing, 1999.

Bessette, Alan E., Arleen R. Bessette, and David W. Fischer. *Mushrooms of Northeastern North America*. New York: Syracuse University Press, 1997.

Fergus, C. Leonard, and Charles Fergus. *Common Edible and Poisonous Mushrooms of the Northeast*. Mechanicsburg, Pa.: Stackpole Press, 2003.

Lincoff, Gary H. *The Audubon Society Field Guide to North American Mushrooms*. New York: Alfred A. Knopf, 1997.

McIlvaine, Charles. *One Thousand American Fungi*. Indianapolis: Bowen-Merrill, 1900.

Smith, Alexander H., Helen V. Smith, and Nancy S. Weber. *How to Know the Gilled Mushrooms*. Dubuque, Iowa: W. C. Brown, 1979.

———. *How to Know the Non-Gilled Mushrooms*. Dubuque, Iowa: W. C. Brown, 1981..

Thomas, William Sturgis. *Field Book of Common Mushrooms*. New York: G. P. Putnam's Sons, 1948.

Index